International Migration: Challenge For The Nineties

Reginald T. Appleyard

PUBLISHED FOR
THE 40TH ANNIVERSARY
OF IOM

IOM International Organization for Migration

IOM
17, route des Morillons
Case postale 71
CH-1211 Genève 19
Switzerland

———

Opinions expressed in this brochure are those of the author.

CONTENTS

FOREWORD

INTRODUCTON   1

SUMMARY   5

CHAPTER 1 - BACKGROUND AND SETTING   11

CHAPTER 2 - WHAT IS HAPPENING?   21

CHAPTER 3 - THE SHORT ROAD AHEAD   63

CHAPTER 4 - THE LONG VIEW   75

Foreword

This Monograph by Professor Appleyard* is an appropriate commemoration of the founding of the International Organization for Migration (IOM), forty years ago. The story of our Organization is also the story of people whose plight has obliged them to seek a new life elsewhere, and in today's changing world, no less than in yesterday's, the issue of migration is a call to participation in problem-solving on a global scale.

In many ways, there are similarities between the year in which IOM was created, 1951, and the year 1991. Not only was 1951 the beginning of a new decade, but it was also a year which opened up perspectives of broad political changes in Europe which would have major influence on world-wide migratory flows.

By 1951, the economies of western European countries were only slowly beginning to recover from the terrible devastation of World War II. Over-population was considered as a restraint on recovery. Italy, in particular, had serious problems of surplus population, given available resources, due to the war-time blockage of its traditional flow of migration to Latin America, and the return of large numbers from former colonies. The Federal Republic of Germany had become self-governing again after adopting a Constitution which guaranteed individual rights under a democratic system. At the same time, Western Germany's industries were only slowly regaining

* Director, Centre for Migration and Development Studies, University of Western Australia.

strength, and in 1951 were unable to provide employment opportunities for all of the manpower among the newly arrived 12 million ethnic Germans who had left their former homes as a result of the Potsdam treaty. In Greece, there was chronic unemployment and a lack of capital investment - conditions which had been aggravated by the post-War civil strife. Conditions of over-population in the Netherlands were also critical, in part because plots of inherited farmlands had become too small to support all members of a family, and because thousands of Dutch had been obliged to return home when Indonesia became independent. Even in Austria, employment possibilities were limited because its economy had been retarded severely by the war, and both agricultural and industrial production were at low levels.

The problems of what were considered surplus populations in the countries just mentioned were regarded, in 1951, as serious threats to their political stability and economic viability. At that point, and by contrast, there were countries outside Europe such as Australia, Canada, the United States, and to a certain extent in Latin America, whose economies had developed intensively to meet war-time production needs, but which were not coping with peace-time needs due to a lack of manpower or, in some instances, population. Against this background, IOM (then known as the Provisional Intergovernmental Committee for the Movement of Migrants from Europe, or PICMME) was created as a temporary international organization to help resolve these population problems - through orderly and planned national and refugee migration.

At the moment of its founding, there were three groups among IOM membership in relation to national migration in particular - namely, emigration countries, immigration countries, and sympathizing countries. The major concern of the so-called sympathizing countries was to establish a successor agency to the International Refugee Organization (IRO) established on 1 July 1947 to deal with the resettlement of refugees from Europe - a subject which had raised controversy within the framework of the United Nations from the very first session of the General Assembly in 1945.

The basic task of IRO had been to assist persons displaced by World War II with special efforts for the victims of concentration or forced labour camps. But with the growing division in Europe, IRO faced the problem of political refugees fleeing their homelands whom some countries of origin considered as political dissidents. The sympathizing States, therefore, decided to dissolve this specialized agency of the United Nations and divide the mandate among three bodies. In 1951, the IRO administration was turned over to local authorities in the countries where the camps were located; international legal protection was entrusted to the newly-formed Office of the United Nations High Commissioner for Refugees (UNHCR); and IOM/PICMME was entrusted with the operational activities involved in the resettlement of displaced persons and refugees. It began its operations in February 1952.

Throughout the 1950s, IOM assisted in developing a flow of national migrants from western Europe mainly to Australia and Canada. In terms of today's world-wide networks of relatively low-cost travel by air, this action by IOM may not seem an achievement. However, in a period of unstable national economies, of widely fluctuating rates for, or even possibilities to, exchange foreign currencies, the work of IOM was essential.

By the end of the decade, IOM had proved its ability to deal with a refugee crisis. In response to an appeal of the Austrian Government to help in the resettlement of Hungarian refugees who had fled from the fighting in Budapest in November 1956, 180,000 Hungarians were resettled from Austria and Yugoslavia.

By the beginning of the 1960s, economic recovery in western Europe had become a booming expansion. Not only was unemployment virtually eliminated, but large-scale inter-European migration was beginning to take place - even from countries such as Yugoslavia and Turkey. Due to these factors, Latin America was an area which was no longer a magnet drawing European workers.

At the same time, Latin American governments reached the conclusion that they were no longer able to absorb large numbers of immigrants or refugees from Europe because of the need to concentrate their efforts on providing employment opportunities for their own increasing populations. Studies were carried out by IOM which pointed out that the growth of the economies of Latin America was hampered by a lack of technical or highly-skilled workers. The *Migration for Development programmes* were thus set up to help developing countries meet those needs by providing highly-skilled personnel unavailable locally.

Throughout the 1960s, IOM proved its value in dealing with a number of critical situations which did not involve refugees in the traditional sense, but provided relief for the distress of persons who had been obliged to flee or had been displaced from their homes by circumstances beyond their control. In a number of instances, this referred to persons obliged to leave former colonial, trust or mandated territories in Africa or the Middle East, as well as minority groups in these areas. Some examples were Belgians (or others) from the Congo; minority groups from Egypt; European nationals from the newly independent countries of Tunisia and Morocco; and Armenians coming into Lebanon from Bulgaria, Romania and Egypt. In all instances, the direct or indirect intervention of IOM as an international migration organization facilitated the orderly resolution of thorny minority questions which might otherwise have become much larger internal or external political, human right or refugee issues. As the decade was ending, this characteristic of IOM as a migration organization again proved its value for the resettlement of some 40,000 Czechoslovaks who fled into Austria, and did not wish to be regarded as political refugees but only as escapees from a foreign intervention.

Early in the decade of the 1970s, IOM initiated a *Return of Talent Programme* to encourage Latin Americans, who had gone abroad for technical training, or for study and experience in scientific fields, to go back to their own countries to contribute towards economic development at home. To stimulate the return of such cases, it was necessary for IOM to identify a specific job opportunity for them, and when necessary, to supplement initial salary scales and social services so that the transition would be less difficult from a more advanced society.

As regards its *refugee migration programmes,* IOM was called on continually throughout the 1970s to handle or assist in various evacuations of individuals caught in crisis situations. The first two were at the request of UNHCR. These involved the repatriation in 1970 to Nigeria of 4,500 children from Biafra, and the return transportation in 1971 of 130,000 persons from Bangladesh and Nepal to Pakistan. An IOM team was sent to Uganda to organize the evacuation of some 5,000 Asians whose expulsion had been ordered to take effect by November 1972.

This was followed by an even more critical situation with the fall of the government of Salvador Allende in Chile. The intervention of IOM began with the clearance of interned foreigners; then, seeking exit permits for Chileans who had sought asylum in foreign embassies and, finally, in assisting those detained or sentenced for political crimes to go into exile - a total of some 29,000 persons over a period of five years. With the collapse of the Cambodian and South Vietnamese Governments in 1975, hundreds of thousands fled to neighbouring countries. Emergency teams were sent by IOM to the affected South East Asian countries in the last half of 1975. By 1976, IOM offices were opened in Indonesia, Malaysia, Singapore and Thailand while the existing office in Hong Kong was strengthened in order to cope with the overwhelming task of resettling Indochinese - a task which continues today.

Entering the 1980s, member-governments began to question the geographical limitations on the work of IOM and the concentration in Europe of its migration programmes, and in 1987, the Council resolved to update its Constitution and to reflect its global activities by a global mandate. As the decade was ending, the Intergovernmental Committee for Migration (ICM) became, in November 1989, the International Organization for Migration (IOM) by the ratification of its amended Constitution.

In the period of this constitutional evolution, IOM programmes were meeting the challenge of achieving new dimensions. First, in 1981, the *Return of Talent Programme* was extended to Latin American nationals residing in the United States, and then, by 1983, this particular programme encompassed African nationals who would return from Europe or the United States to help in the economic development of their home countries. By 1985, migration for development activities were extended to Asia. At this point, IOM also carried out a *Hemispheric Migration Project* to determine the causes and consequences of migration in Latin America and the Caribbean area. After the return to democracy in Argentina, Uruguay and later Chile, IOM began programmes for the return of exiles to these three countries.

Throughout the 1980s, IOM was called on to mount emergency operations for the resettlement of refugees in several parts of the world. First, there was a need to move the thousands of Cubans who had found overcrowded asylum in the Peruvian embassy in Havana. An evacuation was also required for Bolivians detained by military authorities but allowed to go into exile. In Europe, an appeal was received in 1981 from the Austrian Government to help in the emigration overseas of large numbers of Polish asylum seekers who had been able to reach Austria. By 1982, IOM was also operating a special transit facility in Germany to handle the resettlement processing of Polish detainees who had been allowed to go abroad. In the same period, IOM started to provide assistance to Central American refugees and displaced persons in the area so that they could migrate to overseas countries. As an offshoot, IOM implemented a special programme for the emigration from El Salvador of political prisoners and their families who had been amnestied under a decree issued in 1983. On the other side of the world, in South East Asia, IOM had been able to assist in the departure for resettlement of over one million Indochinese refugees. It began to appear at this point that there was a need to care for all those left behind. Special programmes were therefore introduced for handicapped refugees and for long-stayers in camps. However, this prospect changed as the decade of the Nineties opened with waves of new arrivals of boat people.

In the opening year of this decade, IOM was entrusted by the United Nations Disaster Relief Co-ordinator (UNDRO) to organize the repatriation of foreigners stranded in the Gulf region as a consequence of the invasion of Kuwait by Iraq. More than 200,000 foreigners were repatriated under IOM auspices. In the aftermath of the conflict in the Gulf, there still are hundreds of thousands of persons displaced or stranded in the region whom IOM assists as a member of a team of international organizations.

After 40 years in operation, IOM is no longer a temporary organization, and the challenges which it faces now are those which Professor Appleyard has analyzed so cogently in this Monograph.

The main purpose here of reviewing the past is to ascertain that the last 40 years have enriched the Organization with both the operational experiences and perception of migration issues in scope and diversity. "International Migration : Challenge for the Nineties"? Certainly, migration will play a major role at the turn of the twenty first century. The world today faces a host of problems of unprecedented magnitude which very often result in migration. The success or failure to regulate migratory flows will depend on whether the international community has the ability to cope with the main reasons behind migration: poverty and underdevelopment.

The challenge for IOM tomorrow is to find ways to be helpful to governments to ensure that migration be an instrument of development.

James N. Purcell, Jr.
Director General
International Organization
for Migration

IOM publishes this Monograph as a contribution to the ongoing debate, thus fulfilling its mandate to provide a forum for discussion on one of the pressing issues of our time, without taking sides. The debate launched in this volume will continue in the IOM Quarterly *International Migration* of which Professor Appleyard will assume editorship in 1992.

Introduction

Among the topics discussed by the leaders of the most-industrialized nations (G-7) at their recent conference in London was a "growing concern about worldwide migratory pressures".[1/] Although their communiqué did not articulate the nature or causes of these pressures, there is little doubt that the leaders were referring to the widening gap in living standards between countries of the North and the South, limited political freedom and human rights still suffered by many people around the world, and the increasing number of asylum seekers and illegal workers entering countries of the North.

These pressures are increasing at a time when the populations of the North are stable, or in decline, as a result of sustained sub-replacement fertility, whereas the populations of the South are increasing rapidly. While some governments of the North are concerned that the pressures could, in due course, lead to "mass exodus" from the South, few have devised policies that effectively address non-regular types of migration. Indeed, some governments have knowingly admitted illegal migrants to meet unfilled labour demands necessary to service their high rates of economic growth.

Although the viability of the mass-exodus scenario has been questioned on grounds that remedial policies would be in place long before it occurred, little attention has been given to suggesting and debating those policies. Recent international events and altercations which led to, or threatened, unexpected migration, have also been described as straws in the winds of change but, again, little systematic research has been done to assess the relationship between migration and socio-economic change. The events referred to include:

- The Gulf war which forced hundreds of thousands of Arab and Asian workers to return home almost overnight when the Middle East had come to be regarded as an important and stable region for foreign contract employment.

- Increased pressure on eastern Europeans to emigrate to the West following the collapse of communist systems and major changes in the political structure of the Soviet Union. At one stage it was predicted that if exit restrictions were lifted, as many as five million Soviets would try to emigrate westward. [2/]

- Video footage from the Horn of Africa showing that refugee situations of the most appalling kind really do exist in the South, and footage from Bangladesh confirming that the lives of millions of poor people were threatened by a single storm and flood.

There is no doubt that modern communications have made people in the South better informed about lifestyles and opportunities in the North, and modern travel has made it easier for them to go there. Globalisation of economic networks and regional economic blocs have also brought migration (internal as well as international, including migration between South countries) within the reach of many people in the South. International markets and trading systems have also changed so rapidly that many governments have not yet examined the appropriateness of existing migration policies, let alone devised policies that address the emerging pressures referred to by the G-7 leaders.

Policy responses have therefore ranged from those more in tune with Third World aspirations, such as increased intakes of permanent settlers and refugees, to those which permit illegal workers to be deported because they were no longer needed, and refugees to be pushed back to sea in their small and generally unstable craft. Whatever responses governments may make to future straw-in-the-wind occasions, there appears to be a growing consensus that the migratory pressures referred to by G-7 leaders are not illusory, and that appropriate policies designed to facilitate economic growth and preserve political freedom and human rights are the most effective ways of reducing such pressures.

Emigration pressure is, of course, relative; there have always been, and still are, millions of persons ready to move to countries with higher standards of living and fairer political systems. Pressure is normally strongest in countries at the deprivation end of the income and political freedom/human rights spectrum. The two circumstances are not unconnected. Pioneering work by Aristide Zolberg and his colleagues on the causes of refugee and irregular migration show that different types of social conflict give rise to different types of refugee flows and that the patterns of conflict are themselves intimately related to general economic and political conditions. They contend that in the developing world, where almost all the world's refugees live, regimes come and go (e.g., civilian or military, democratic or authoritarian), whereas the conflicts that produce this instability are themselves enduring.[3/]

Persons suffering severe poverty are generally more likely to stay put until near-starvation overtakes and they struggle to move elsewhere probably, as in the case of Africa, to a nearby country not much better off than their own. Such persons, it has been argued, pose no migration threat to countries of the North: distance, inability to finance travel and fear of the unknown combine to prevent them from becoming part of a mass exodus. Greater pressure is expected to come from compatriots in better economic circumstances, or from persons in countries higher up the international per capita GNP ladder, who are ambitious, know where the opportunities exist, can raise the travel costs and, if necessary, will risk arrest in a country of the North knowing that their deportation is unlikely. Persons with these characteristics appear to typify the increasing asylum-seeker and illegal populations in countries of the North.

For these and other reasons, the causes and consequences of present and future international migration are now being more widely and vigorously discussed than ever before. This monograph, sponsored by the International Organization for Migration, attempts to assess the volume, direction and composition of contemporary international migration with a view to assessing whether, as has been claimed, the conditions for mass migration are steadily developing. Likely trends in volume and composition of migration during the next few years are also suggested. And on the grounds that income differentials between countries of the North and South (an accepted primary cause of mass migration) are both wide or widening, global economic policies designed to reduce the differentials are proposed and discussed.

NOTES

1.
Daily Telegraph, 18 July 1991.

2.
In addressing the abruptness of East-West détente, Papademetriou argued that the West was caught off-balance without an adequate analytical paradigm. Without it, he concluded, we can expect to continue to witness a large degree of confusion and wasted effort. See Demetrios G. Papademetriou, "Confronting the Challenge of Transnational Migration: Domestic and International Responses", a paper presented at the OECD International Conference on Migration, Rome, March 1991, p. 2.

3.
Aristide R. Zolberg, Astri Suhrke and Sergio Aguayo, ***Escape from Violence. Conflict and the Refugee Crisis in the Developing World,*** Oxford University Press, New York.

Summary

An assessment of contemporary migration has shown that developing countries have been increasingly drawn into global networks. As many as 70 million persons, mostly from developing countries, are either working (legally and illegally) in other countries, over one million persons emigrate permanently to other countries each year, close to an equal number seek asylum and over twelve million refugees live outside their homelands compared with about two million in the 1950s.

Though countries in western Europe may well be receiving more "immigrants" than the United States, the former do not readily acknowledge that they are, or have become, countries of immigration. The traditional receivers (United States, Canada and Australia), however, are declared countries of immigration in the sense that they share a fundamental belief in its value for nation-building. Their intakes of permanent immigrants have been maintained at high levels, and diverse ethnic compositions, fortified by family reunification, have led to very high proportions being drawn from developing countries. On the other hand, Latin America, once a traditional receiver, now attracts few immigrants from other regions and is losing highly-skilled and professional workers to the United States and Canada and, more recently, to European "ethnic" homelands. Latin America's main migration flows are now intra-regional, between countries at different levels of economic prosperity.

Recent patterns of migration in East and South East Asia have been greatly influenced by the high rates of economic growth and rapid movement through demographic transition of Japan and the "four dragons" (Taiwan, South Korea, Hong Kong and

Singapore). These countries have obtained migrant labour, but not permanent migrants, from nearby countries at earlier stages of transition (e.g., the Philippines, Thailand and Indonesia) which are also important providers of contract labour to the Middle East. All countries in East and South East Asia, with the exception of Japan, have also supplied permanent migrants to the traditional receivers. This complex pattern of migration in a rapidly changing region can be partly explained by the application of a model based upon the concept of demographic transition. Countries at early stages of modernisation (the horizontal axis in transition - see Figure 1, p.18) typically lose large numbers of emigrants to countries at later stages, although composition according to type of migration (permanent, contract labour, professional transient, illegal/clandestine and refugee) varies at each stage of transition. Immigration, on the other hand, increases with modernisation, especially when, as in the case of the newly-industrialized countries (NICs) in Asia demographic transition occurs within a very short period. Governments decide the numbers and composition of immigration (including type) on the basis of their plans for socio-economic development. Immigration requirements, in terms of numbers, type and composition, vary according to the stage of modernisation reached by each country.

In addition to receiving a large number of contract workers from Asia, the Middle East has also been a moderate supplier of permanent emigrants to the traditional receivers. Israel dominates the region's permanent immigration statistics and, in response to major political changes in the Soviet Union, is admitting an increasing number of Jews from what, in reality, is the last remaining major source.

South Asia and sub-Saharan Africa are the regions where severe emigration pressures are considered most likely to gather. Numbers of emigrants (both contract worker and permanent) from South Asia are, however, minuscule relative to the region's estimated population of over one billion. Sub-Saharan Africa has provided few contract workers to other regions and most of its refugees have been resettled within the region. Available data indicate diverse rates of economic growth, but poverty, underemployment, unemployment, poor services and infrastructure characterise sub-Saharan Africa as a whole. Emigration to other regions is mainly by skilled and professional workers, and intra-African flows are to countries with the highest real incomes and rates of economic growth: Nigeria in the west and the Republic of South Africa in the south. In the absence of even basic information on flows, it has not been possible to convey anything more than general trends, although the continent appears to be experiencing large flows of contract worker and illegal migration. Refugee populations are, in aggregate, the largest in the world.

Despite overall dearth of data, notably on South Asia and sub-Saharan Africa, short-term migration projections for each region were attempted on the grounds that most migration, including some illegal, remains firmly under the control of receiving governments, and that many of the factors that will shape the world economy during the next decade are already in train or are otherwise sufficiently predetermined to indicate how they will unfold.

The immigration issue will become even more important in the labour market of the European Community (EC), increasingly dominated by service and information technologies. Governments of ageing, prosperous economies will have to decide whether to try and meet demand for appropriately-skilled labour by implementing policies directed towards internal restructuring (including retraining and higher participation rates), or to admit immigrants with appropriate skills on short-term contracts. Most EC governments will probably opt for both.

These policies would, however, do little to reduce emigration pressures that are strong and increasing in such nearby regions as eastern Europe and the southern Mediterranean. Both regions offer investment opportunities that should lead to job creation, but potential emigration from eastern Europe (due to ethnic regrouping, political exodus and economic migration for survival) is numbered in the millions. Population projections for the southern Mediterranean indicate spectacular rates of growth during the next thirty years. A major issue for the European Community is the extent to which it is prepared to draw on these regions for appropriately-skilled labour and, if intake is to be limited, how it will control the expected large numbers of asylum seekers and illegal workers. Policy implementation will therefore be just as important as policy-making during the remainder of the 1990s.

The traditional receivers have already set immigration targets for the next five or so years. Large family reunion components will be filled by ethnics from those developing countries which provided the majority of each receiving-country's recent immigrants. However, the salient feature of each of the traditional receivers' future programmes is to increase substantially the number of Independent (mainly highly-skilled) immigrants. Given the expected strengthening of tripolars, namely, the emerging economic blocs in Europe, Asia/Pacific and America, and the likely increase in demand for skilled workers in other regions, the OECD continous reporting system on migration (known under its french acronym SOPEMI) rightly asks whether we are about to see "fierce competition on a worldwide scale to secure the most highly-skilled workers".

Unless Latin America's economic growth rates improve substantially, loss of migrants to other regions is unlikely to be arrested during the 1990s. The United States and Europe will remain magnets for migrants, especially those who are skilled and professional, and there is unlikely to be much change in the established pattern of intra-regional migration between countries at different stages of modernisation.

East and South East Asia are growing so rapidly that migration flows, even in the short term, are difficult to assess and predict. Researchers are now obliged to rely upon newspapers for reports of new and unexpected migration flows in the region. Because rates of economic growth in Japan and the "four dragons" are unlikely to decline in the near future, demand for migrant labour will almost certainly increase. Japan, the region's economic linchpin, only recently opened its doors to foreign workers, but an unexpected high incidence of illegal unskilled workers resulted in legislation that imposed heavy penalties on such persons, as well as on their employers. In many respects, Japan, with its ageing sub-replacement population, faces dilemmas similar to those facing the European Community. Its policies for the near future, despite a projected labour shortfall of over two million by the year 2000, will probably be a mix of capital-intensive domestic production, increased workforce participation rates and the export of jobs to nearby countries.

Toe-holds established in the labour markets of East and South East Asia by legal and illegal workers from South Asia are unlikely to be relinquished. Contract labour emigration to the Middle East from established Asian sources will also continue even though numbers have declined during the last few years, and the Gulf crisis has certainly destabilised the market. However, oil-producing countries operate their contract labour programmes in a buyer's market and there will be no shortage of supply. Skill composition of intakes has already changed and countries with appropriate workers will obtain a higher share of the market than those without.

South Asia and sub-Saharan Africa are the world's poorest regions whose constituent countries are at mid- or early stages of demographic transition. Opportunities for migration from both regions to the tripolars will be limited. Some skilled and professional workers will emigrate (together with contract workers from South Asia to the Middle East), but numbers will be minuscule relative to the large and rapidly-growing populations. In the absence of appropriate global economic policies, their worsening predicaments will lead to increased conflict and instability and therefore an increased incidence of refugee situations.

This Monograph argues that wide and widening income differentials between North and South can be narrowed only by economic policies initiated by the North and directed towards economic and social development of the South. An appropriate policy package would include a strengthened and extended multilateral trading system (that need not necessarily be retarded by activities of the tripolars), rescheduling and selected forgiveness of accumulated debt (which in turn would attract foreign investment) and carefully-devised co-operative aid programmes. Equally important would be that countries of the South try and create stable macro-economic environments. Indeed, many economists deem this a *necessary* condition for economic growth.

Should such a policy package be implemented, international migration would occur in response to socio-economic growth, not as mass exodus or loss of selected workers from developing countries as a result of deteriorating economic conditions. However, from what we know concerning the relationship between migration and economic growth - and it is precious little - rapid and successful development is likely to be profoundly disturbing to developing countries in the short-term. The US Commission for the Study of International Migration and Co-operative Economic Development bluntly predicted that with an appropriate development strategy in place, migration between South and North in the short term would increase rather than moderate. But this would be a small price to pay if, in the long run, it obviated mass exodus with all its accompanying conflict and dislocation.

This monograph has not addressed many important consequential aspects of the development strategy option, including exploitation of resources (renewable and non-renewable) and the environmental consequences of a world containing over 11 billion people enjoying an overall higher standard of living. These issues need to be addressed as a matter of urgency. No less urgent is the need for more research, dialogue and action on what Jonas Widgren describes as the linkage between large-scale internal and international migration, population increase, regional inequality and global security.

1

Background and Setting

Although international migration has been an integral and abiding part of human history and achievement, its alleged capacity to dislocate and change economic and social systems within a short period has only recently become an issue of major international concern. During the nineteenth century, when the world's population was less than two billion, most of the important migration flows were initiated by colonial powers and by governments of the then so-called traditional receivers - the United States, Canada, Australia, New Zealand, Argentina, Brazil, South Africa and Rhodesia. Colonial powers were responsible for an estimated 15 million slaves being transported from Africa for work in the Americas prior to 1850,[1] and during the century following the official end of slavery (i.e., from 1834 to 1937), over 30 million persons were shifted from the Indian sub-continent to work in other colonies in Asia, the Indian Ocean and the Caribbean, although about 24 million ultimately returned home. Though not designated slaves, Lord John Russell described their conditions as indentured servitude. In eastern Asia, as a consequence of labour migrations of a similar kind, Chinese populations in Hong Kong, Indonesia, Thailand and Malaysia exceeded 16 million by the end of the Second World War.[2] An estimated 50 million Europeans simultaneously emigrated to the traditional receivers between 1846 and 1924.[3]

The Second World War is generally considered to have been a watershed in global migration. With the departure of colonial powers during the 1940s and 1950s, new independent governments set about devising economic and population (including migration) policies to facilitate *their* objectives, not those of former colonial masters. Changes in the immigration policies of traditional receivers just prior to World War II had also brought to an end the relatively free flow of Europeans to those countries. Acts passed in the United States during the 1920s had restricted intakes and allocated quotas to mainly European countries; and the Empire Settlement Act of 1922 encouraged (and financially assisted) Britons to emigrate to the Dominions as one way of countering the growing influence of US traders in Britain's overseas markets.[4/]

The devastation created in Europe by the Second World War saw more than a million or more displaced persons, mainly from central and eastern Europe, resettle in the traditional receiving-countries and hundreds of thousands of western Europeans emigrate under bilateral agreements. Emigration-mindedness was also very strong; long queues of potential emigrants stretched from the doors of the United States, Canadian and Australian embassies throughout Europe. Indeed, the Government of the Netherlands actively encouraged some of its people to emigrate as a contribution towards alleviating the country's perceived "population problem"; and in the United Kingdom, opinion polls revealed that one quarter or more of the population would emigrate if free to do so.

But European economic recovery was not long in coming, and with it came a marked decline in emigration mindedness. By the early 1960s, the Federal Republic of Germany had achieved its celebrated economic miracle which not only reduced emigration pressures but led to a substantial demand for foreign workers to satisfy a rapidly increasing demand for labour. Northern Europe as a whole ultimately invited ten million guest workers (and their dependants) from Mediterranean countries as well as an additional two million workers from former colonies.[5/] As described by Rudiger Soltwedel, the period from 1950 to the first oil-price shock in 1973 was a golden age, the heyday of Europe's economic growth when real gross domestic product (GDP) increased by nearly 5 per cent a year in the countries of the Organization for Economic Co-operation and Development (OECD).[6/] This was also the period when it was confidently expected that the entry of large numbers of workers from southern Europe would, through remittances, reduced unemployment and underemployment, investment and higher purchasing power, initiate economic development in southern Europe. While no one doubts the enormous changes that have occurred in southern Europe's economic development (making Italy, for example, a country of net immigration), some scholars still doubt the role played by guest-worker emigration in that achievement.[7]

Although the first oil-price shock marked the end of Europe's post-war golden age, and led to restrictions on immigration, numbers increased again during the early 1980s despite recruitment bans. Demand for unskilled foreign industrial labour declined mainly as a result of automation in production, but demand for workers to fill low-paid jobs in other sectors increased, leading to a marked increase in illegal immigration. Italy, Spain and Greece, which had provided a large proportion of northern Europe's guest workers, now host probably a million illegal migrants from non-European bordering countries.[8] Situations such as these have introduced what Georges Tapinos calls a complex and contradictory set of factors into the immigration issue, including a fear that any extension of illegal immigration could cause a breakdown in social and political equilibrium.[9]

The 1960s were also a golden age for the traditional receivers when immigrants from Europe provided much-needed labour to service high rates of economic growth. It also saw traditional receivers such as the United States, Canada and Australia change their immigration policies, which hitherto had strongly favoured Europeans, to admit persons with proven skills and achievements, whatever their ethnicity. These new policies were directly responsible for a significant braindrain from both Europe and Third World countries. Policies sympathetic to non-European refugees, especially from Indochina following the Vietnam conflict, and in particular policies sympathetic to family reunion, contributed to a remarkable change in the ethnic composition of immigration to the traditional receivers. By 1985-1989, 90 per cent of immigrants to the United States were from developing countries and an equal percentage had gained entry as beneficiaries of a US citizen or permanent resident. In Canada, three out of five landed immigrants between 1985 and 1987 were from developing countries as were five out of ten settlers to Australia between 1985 and 1988.[10] The impact of immigration policies that favoured highly-skilled and professional workers is reflected in the US census of 1980 which showed that 80 per cent of workers born in India were in "professional, technical and kindred" occupations.

While buoyant economies, high economic growth and per capita incomes characterized western Europe and the traditional receivers for most of the post-war period, stagnation, high rates of population growth and low per capita incomes characterized many of the newly-independent developing countries of the South. The term *South* is roughly synonymous with *developing country* although it must be emphasized that both appellations encompass diverse economic and demographic situations. Some countries, notably the NICs of East and South East Asia, now have rates of economic growth and per capita incomes similar to some countries of the North. For most of the South, however, per capita income is not only low but unevenly distributed.

Understanding processes of socio-economic change, especially in countries of the South, has been facilitated by the concept of demographic transition which applies to all countries as they move from low to high stages of economic development. Transition occurs over four stages of modernization represented by the horizontal axis in Figure 1 (see page 18); from high birth and high death rates during the first stage to low birth and low death rates during the fourth stage. Population growth is therefore low at these two stages because birth and death rates cancel out. At the middle stages of transition, when birth rates have declined only slightly but death rates markedly, population growth is high. Although net migration, the other determinant of population growth, can have a significant impact on rates of overall growth, it normally does not exercise much influence, either positive or negative, in countries of the South during the middle stages of transition.

Among countries presently in the middle, high growth, stages of transition are such demographic heavyweights as India, Pakistan, Bangladesh and a number of countries in sub-Saharan Africa. Present annual rates of population growth in Africa as a whole are 3 per cent and 2.1 per cent in South Asia. In 35 years, Latin America's population is projected to exceed 750 million, that of South Asia 2.2 billion and that of Africa 1.6 billion.[11/] High rates of growth in large, mid-transition populations are largely responsible for present high rates of global population growth. The present world population of 5.6 billion (1990) is therefore expected to reach 11 billion by the third quarter of the 21st century when an overwhelming proportion of people will be living in what we presently identify as developing countries (Figure 2, see page 19). How rapidly these countries proceed through transition will depend almost entirely upon their rates of economic growth or modernisation.

Demographic trends in countries of the South have placed enormous strains on their governments' capacity to provide education, social security and, especially, jobs. Antonio Golini's research has strikingly highlighted orders of magnitude *vis-à-vis* countries that have already gone through demographic transition. He shows that in European OECD countries there are 13 children under 15 years for every ten persons over 65 years; in sub-Saharan Africa there are 159 children for every ten old persons. Thus, the expected *increase* in numbers of persons of labour-force ages in less-developed countries during the next 20 years is 733 million compared with the *present* labour force in developed countries of 586 million. This means that developing countries have the capability of employing in only 20 years an additional number of workers much greater than the 1990 stock of the whole developed world.[12/] Population growth and young age structures will therefore provoke an unprecedented growth differential in workforces of the South compared with those of the North. In the early 1990s, many European countries are expected to achieve population growth rates of only 0.5 per cent and by 2025 be declining or growing only slowly.[13/]

These estimates indicate the magnitude of potential "mass migration". Of equal importance, of course, is the extent to which the large number of persons of working age in developing countries will be likely to find jobs there. The prognosis is not favourable. Present high and increasing rates of unemployment and underemployment, typically weak resource bases, low productivity, high external debt and difficulty of access to world markets have combined to stabilize or even depress low rates of economic growth in many countries of the South. Indeed, economic differentials between South and North are as striking in their magnitude as are the demographic differentials. Louis Emmerij quotes figures showing that average annual per capita income of "low-income countries" increased from $140 in 1965 to $270 by the beginning of the 1980s whereas the increase in industrial countries was from $8,800 to $14,400. Furthermore, by the late 1980s, per capita income in developing countries had slipped back to end-1970s levels, "thus regressing each year over the last decade".[14/]

It is therefore not surprising that many influential scholars and administrators have concluded that, in the absence of appropriate global economic policies, differentials of these magnitudes are unlikely to narrow. Migratory pressures are therefore likely to increase during the coming decades. For example, James N. Purcell, the Director General of the International Organization for Migration, has warned that when economic stagnation or a sharp fall in incomes further aggravates the deprivation of vast numbers of less-privileged people in the South, generating a feeling of despair and hopelessness, then mass migration, legal or illegal, could occur.[15/] *The Human*

Development Report for 1991 concluded that because the pressures for international migration are building rapidly, the next decade could see unprecedented movements across international borders exceeding migration from Europe to the United States, Canada and Australia.[16] And Jonas Widgren has argued strongly that mass movements of people between South and North will inevitably occur as a result of population pressures and economic imbalances.[17] The potential for migration, he wrote, is steadily building. Most waves to developed countries will probably develop gradually and according to highly-predictable, long-established regional problems, building upon the established network of South-North movements. The accumulated effect of these movements in a decade or two, he argued, will be tremendous.[18]

If Widgren is correct, and these migration waves are already gathering, then reversal will be difficult to achieve. Larger, poorer populations in countries of the South will also place at risk ecological systems and capacity to increase agricultural output. In this regard, the projection of the Food and Agriculture Organization of the United Nations (FAO) that 65 per cent of the world's non-irrigated agricultural acreage will be uncultivable by the year 2100 should be heeded.[19]

NOTES

1.
Sergio Ricca, ***International Migration in Africa. Legal and Administrative Aspects***, ILO, Geneva, 1989, p. 10.

2.
Reginald T. Appleyard, "International Migration in Asia and the Pacific", ***International Migration Today,*** Vol. 1, Trends and Prospects, UNESCO, Paris and University of Western Australia, Nedlands, 1988, pp. 106-19; I.S. Gilani, ***Citizens, Slaves, Guest Workers,*** Institute of Policy Studies, Islamabad, 1985.

3.
Maurice R. Davie, ***World Immigration***, New York, 1949, p. 9.

4.
Reginald T. Appleyard, ***British Emigration to Australia,*** Weidenfeld and Nicolson, London, 1964.

5.
S. Castles, ***Here for Good: Western Europe's New Ethnic Minorities,*** London, 1984.

6.
Rudiger Soltwedel, "Structural Adjustment, Economic Growth and Employment", a paper presented at the OECD International Conference on Migration, Rome, March 1991, p. 4.

7.
G. Tapinos, ***L'économie des migrations internationales***, Armand Colin, Paris, 1974.

8.
Jonas Widgren, "International Migration and Regional Stability," ***International Affairs,*** Vol. 66, No. 4, Oct. 1990, p. 753.

9. Georges Tapinos, " Can International Co-operation be an Alternative to the Emigration of Workers?", a paper presented at the OECD International Conference on Migration, Rome, March 1991, p. 5.

10. H. Zlotnik, "Trends in South to North Migration: The Perspective from the North", *International Migration,* Vol. XXIX, No. 2, June 1991, pp. 318-19 and Table 2.

11. N. Sadik, *The State of World Population 1990,* New York, UN Population Fund, 1990.

12. Antonio Golini, *et al.,* "Population Vitality and Decline: The North-South Contrast", a paper presented to the OECD International Conference on Migration, Rome, March 1991, p.9; A. Golini, *et al.,* "South-North Migration with Special Reference to Europe," *International Migration,* Vol. XXIX, No. 2, June 1991, p. 255.

13. United Nations, *World Population Prospects 1990,* New York, 1991.

14. Louis J. Emmerij, "The International Situation, Economic Development and Employment", a paper presented to the OECD International Conference on Migration, Rome, March 1991, p. 6.

15. J. N. Purcell, Jr., Opening Address, *International Migration,* **Vol. XXIX,** No. 2, June 1991, p. 158.

16. UNDP (United Nations Development Programme), *Human Development Report 1991,* New York, Oxford University Press, New York, 1991, p. 80.

17. Jonas Widgren, "Movements of Refugees and Asylum-Seekers: Recent Trends in a Comparative Perspective", a paper presented to the OECD International Conference on Migration, Rome, March 1991, p. 4.

18. Jonas Widgren (1990), p. 761.

19. Swedish Ministry of Labour, *A Comprehensive Refugee and Immigration Policy,* Swedish Government Printer, Stockholm, 1990, pp. 20-1.

Figure 1

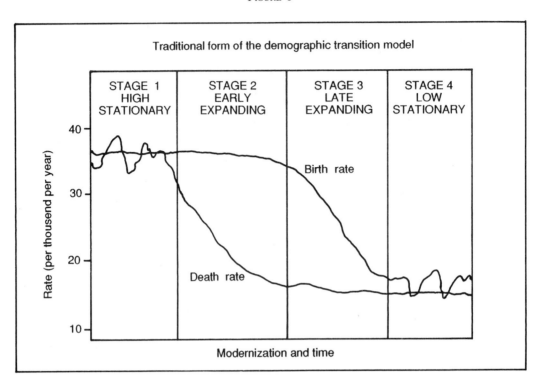

FIGURE 2
PROJECTED WORLD POPULATION

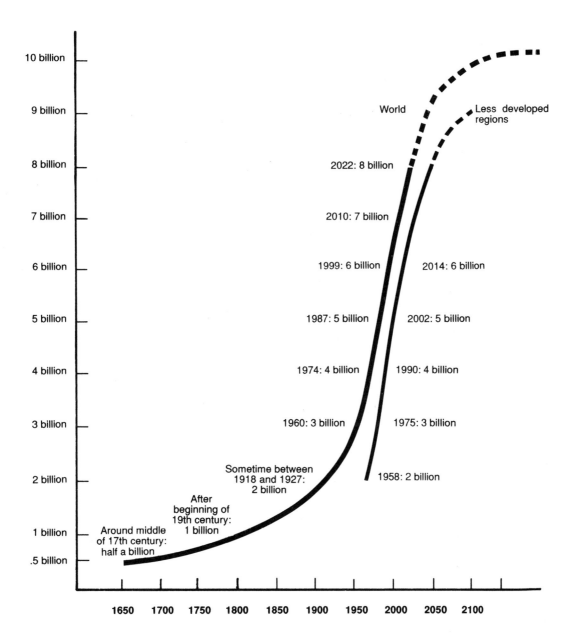

NOTE: Graph is partially based on figures which are derived from medium variant projections. Graph does not necessarily depict what will happen in the furure. It only illustrates what could happen under certain assumptions of fertility and mortality. Curves have been manually extrapolated beyond 2025.

Source: R. M. Salas, *The State of World Population*, UNFPA, 1987, page 2.

2

What is happening?

Although the economic differentials (and in some places political freedom and human rights) separating South and North are probably already wide enough to initiate mass migration, irregular-type migration has in fact been quite limited. Countries of the South have certainly become increasingly involved in migration to the North, as well as in migration to other countries of the South, in what Demetrios Papademetriou has aptly described as a widening and a deepening of the reach of the migration process,[1/] but much of it has been formally controlled by receiving governments under existing immigration regulations. Even so, international migration has been changing considerably in character during the last five to ten years, especially the increasing convergence of refugee and economically motivated migration.[2/] New, unexpected groups keep coming up which need to be dealt with, such as the displaced, exiles, poverty affected, unique humanitarian cases, environmental refugees and asylees, "exceptions", which James N. Purcell suggests too often become permanent. Regulatory systems are therefore becoming harder to understand, articulate and administer. Furthermore, he wrote, existing migration mechanisms are ill-suited to cope with tomorrow's - or for that matter today's - migration realities.[3/]

To ill-suited mechanisms must also be added inadequate information. Trying to tabulate and assess the volume, direction and composition of all types of migration to and from over 150 countries when even definitions are not compatible, and governments not always able or willing to provide required data, becomes something of an analytical nightmare. While researchers cannot, and should not, expect reams of information that cannot be put to good use, the fact of the matter is that basic, priority data for many important migration countries are simply not available. If an adequate response is to be made to the G-7 leaders' concern about growing worldwide migratory pressures, much more basic data on flows and a clearer understanding of why flows and their compositions are changing, will be needed.

The salient feature of regular (i.e., excluding illegal) immigration is that *receiving* governments decide numbers and composition. Millions of persons may wish to emigrate from a poor to a prosperous country, but achieved flows will comprise only those persons whom the government of the latter country is prepared to accept, including the dependents of "prime" migrants. A migrant's acceptability will depend, to a large extent, upon whether he/she is likely to contribute to the receiving country's socio-economic development. The receiving-country's specific requirements will therefore depend upon its stage of economic development, or modernization (Figure 1).

Elsewhere, I have argued that total emigration is likely to be high at early stages of transition but decline as a country approaches final stages, whereas immigration is likely to be negligible at early stages and increase with modernization.[4/] Such a proposition, however, is of little value in either explaining migratory flows at any particular stage or of being a useful predictor of future migration flows. The generalization does however become more useful if migration flows are disaggregated according to the various types. Widgren is even more explicit, arguing that it is necessary at the international level to distinguish clearly between types of migration in order to address adequately the causes of potential mass movements.[5/]

A widely accepted typology of international migration identifies:

- *permanent (settlers)*, including persons admitted under family reunion schemes;

- *temporary contract workers*, normally semi-skilled or unskilled who remain in the receiving-country for finite periods, often two years;

- *temporary professional transients*, professional or skilled workers who move from one country to another usually as employees of international and/or joint venture companies;

- *clandestine or illegal workers* whose entry may or may not be sanctioned by the receiving-country's government;

- *asylum seekers* who cross borders and appeal for status on grounds of political discrimination; and

- *refugees* as defined by the 1951 UN Convention relating to the Status of Refugees.

Explanation of the composition of immigration and emigration during the transition is as follows: concerning *immigration*, a country at the first stage of transition would be unlikely to need (and therefore unlikely to attract) permanent settlers or temporary contract and illegal workers. If its ample supply of low-cost labour attracts foreign investment, then the factory being built or the resource being exploited would almost certainly need the services and advice of professional transients. Although asylum seekers and refugees would probably not enter the country during early stages of transition, this would depend to a large extent upon political circumstances in their homelands. It should be noted that most refugee populations are in developing countries and the circumstances which cause these situations are usually a complex mix of political, economic and social conditions. Case studies conducted by Zolberg and his colleagues in sub-Saharan Africa, the Horn, South Asia and other regions at early stages of transition, show that patterns of conflict which lead to refugee situations are intimately related to more general economic and political considerations.[6/] Refugees are therefore likely to move *from* countries at early stages of transition to countries at similar stages and even experience economic conditions inferior to those in the countries that they left behind.

If a country moves rapidly through transition, experiencing high rates of economic growth (modernization), as have Singapore, Hong Kong and Taiwan, labour supply may soon have to be supplemented by foreign contract, and even illegal, workers. Professional transients would also arrive in increasing numbers. At the final stage of transition, a country is not only likely to require a sustained supply of workers because sub-replacement fertility has reduced its own supply, but also offer permanent residence to highly skilled and professional migrants and their dependants. Immigrants could even include former citizens who left the country during an early stage of transition as part of the brain drain. A country at the final stage would also be more likely to extend permanent settlement rights to refugees and to attract asylum seekers, including those whose appeals were based mainly upon economic deprivation in the homeland.

Governments have less control over *emigration*. The main impediment to outflow is that a potential emigrant must have found a country willing to accept them, either on a permanent or temporary basis. Losses at early stages of transition would therefore include many professional and highly skilled workers going to developed countries (the braindrain), including students studying abroad who fail to return. The country would also be a reservoir for contract and illegal labour emigration. And if political freedom and human rights are limited, which they often are in countries at early stages of transition, then the outflow would also include asylum seekers and refugees. With modernization, incentive for permanent emigration recedes as does contract/illegal worker emigration because of local job creation. If the country's education and training systems have improved, there may also be some loss of persons who join the ranks of professional transients. There is also less likelihood of emigration occurring because of limited political freedom or human rights.

Although the model fits reasonably well the experiences of a number of small countries which have moved rapidly through transition,[7] its applicability to the demographic heavyweights moving slowly through transition is yet to be tested. Nonetheless, disaggregation of the migration phenomenon, together with clear recognition that receiving governments decide both numbers and composition of all types of legal, and even some illegal, immigration, provides a solid foundation on which to try and explain and assess global migration trends.

Dearth of data imposes serious restrictions on the assessment of volume and composition of current migration flows although it is possible to plug some gaps in the estimates of outward flows with data on inward flows provided by countries with superior data. Estimates of legal flows are obviously more reliable than those of illegal flows. Although it is desirable, though not always possible, to separate clearly estimates of "stocks" from estimates of "flows", one often finds it necessary to utilize both. One must also learn to live with the problems posed by "category jumpers", persons who appear in immigration statistics as, say, settler arrivals but who, after a short period, change their minds and leave the country.

Despite these difficulties, it is possible, by utilising and comparing a number of sources, to reach general estimates of current migration trends. Probably in excess of one million persons settled *permanently* in other countries, mainly the traditional receivers, during 1990. The International Labour Organisation (ILO) estimated the total *migrant labour* force in the same year as 25 million,[8/] similar to another estimate of 25 to 30 million, (including illegals but excluding refugee workers), made for 1980.[9/] Widgren also calculated that in 1990 there were at least six million foreigners currently employed in the European labour market, five million in the Middle East and a similar number in the United States though he declined to make estimates for other regions, including sub-Saharan Africa and Asia.[10/] Given the nature of their activities, it is difficult to assess the flow of *professional transients*. Some may already be included in migrant-labour estimates and it is not uncommon for some transients to make several moves each year while others may stay for a year or more in one place accompanied by their families. The number could well exceed half a million. Likewise, it is difficult, for obvious reasons, to assess the number of *illegal* migrants. IOM has suggested not only that it could be in the order of 30 million and that most come from poor countries.[11/] The world's *refugee* population has been estimated by UNHCR at 12 million, having risen from two million in the 1950s. If internal displaced persons are added, the current number could be as high as 26 million.[12/]

CURRENT MIGRATION TRENDS

The above estimates, an unfortunate but necessary mix of stocks and flows from sources of variable quality, are nonetheless sufficient, when supplemented with data from national statistical sources, to provide a broad-brush picture of current migration trends.

The United States, Canada and Australia, with high per capita incomes and long traditions of immigration, continue to accept a large proportion of the world's *permanent immigrants*. These include highly skilled and professional workers from countries at early stages of transition as well as refugees who entered under special permanent-settlement programmes. Numbers have been considerably supplemented by relatives arriving under family-reunion programmes. Western Europe, also a high per-capita-income post-transition region, has become a destination for many immigrants, although it is not clear whether the category "immigrant" (which includes persons who plan to stay for specified periods) also covers asylum seekers who were granted status or, in the case of the Federal Republic of Germany, whether all ethnic German immigrants had the right to German citizenship. However, according to Hania Zlotnik's estimates, the annual average intake of immigrants to Belgium, the Federal Republic of Germany, the Netherlands, Sweden and the United Kingdom between 1985 and 1988 was 240,000, about half of whom were from developing countries.[13/] Demetrios Papademetriou describes European industrial democracies as "immigration countries of great significance" and, depending upon the accounting method used, numbers may be far closer to North American totals than usually thought.[14/]

The flow of *contract-labour migration* is greater and much more widely dispersed than permanent migration, being used by many countries to supplement local labour supplies during periods of high economic growth. Its globalization, aptly described by José N. Sarmiento as a "feature of our times",[15/] has seen many countries "buying" man-hours, (i.e., preferring to pay for a rotating stock of temporary labour whose demands on social expenditures are small compared with permanent migrants).[16/] In sub-Saharan Africa, the flow of contract workers between countries at different stages of modernization has been, and remains, substantial. According to Aderanti Adepoju, many governments see it as a safety valve.[17/] Labour migration also occurs in South America between countries at different stages of development. It must be acknowledged, however, that South-South flows often relate to complex national movements which are domestic rather than international, thereby making explanation harder to fathom.[18/]

The flow of Arab and Asian workers to Middle East oil-producing countries is still substantial, even though skill-composition has changed and there has been a rapid increase in migration between countries in Asia. Its direction is mainly from countries at middle and low stages of transition to Japan and the so-called "four dragons".

Professional transients, in many respects a special type of contract worker, are associated mainly with employment in multinational enterprises (MNEs). ILO estimates that in 1986 approximately 65 million persons were employed by MNEs worldwide, of whom 22 million were employed outside their home country: 18 per cent in Latin America, 13 per cent in Asia and 2 per cent in Africa.[19/] Although probably only a small proportion of these persons were professional transients, the figures nonetheless emphasise the importance of the role being played by professional transients in processes of global development. Numbers have almost certainly increased significantly during the last few years as international companies have further globalized their production techniques and marketing strategies.[20]

The flow and direction of *illegal migration*, together with asylum seekers, is a sensitive index of "migration pressure" even though difficulties of entry may not be great if the receiving country needs workers to fill jobs for which local labour is unavailable. The Mexico-United States flow was for many years the most celebrated example of illegal migration. Despite a 1986 legislation programme by the United States which "discovered" more than three million illegals, it is reckoned "that there are now again about three million clandestine aliens there".[21] Nor does it appear that employer sanctions have greatly influenced the social mechanism that facilitates unauthorized migration. In Latin America, the proportion of illegal migrants, usually not counted in censuses, is "significantly high".[22] In Europe the population of illegal migrants has been estimated at between 1.3 and 1.5 million and expected to reach three million by the year 2000.[23] Most are located in Italy, Spain, Portugal and Greece. A high proportion are overstayers, aged under 40 years, who have been absorbed into ethnic communities and are working in labour-intensive industries with "unsocial working conditions". As in the United States, regularization programmes in Italy have not only uncovered a large number of illegals, whose numbers will be supplemented through family reunion.[24] The "sonatoria" conducted in Italy in 1990 revealed 223,000 illegals, mainly from North Africa and Asia,[25] which was much fewer than the estimated 800,000 undocumented migrants assumed to have been in the country at the time.[26] In eastern Europe, the new democracies (Hungary, Poland and Czechoslovakia) have to cope not only with the emigration of their own people to the west, but also with illegal immigrants, estimated as high as 100,000, from Romania, the Middle East and Soviet states.[27] Asia's high economic growth rates have also led to illegal populations of about one million in Malaysia and 300,000 in Japan. These situations are selected for illustration; the illegal phenomenon is well established, and numbers are increasing, in all parts of the world.

An increase in the number of *asylum seekers* in European countries from 68,700 in 1983 to 401,500 in 1990,[28] though still numerically small, has caused great concern in receiving countries because such a method of entry represents an effective way of by-passing formal immigration regulations. Indeed, it has been estimated that the annual State costs associated with controlling the asylum-seeker phenomenon in western Europe ($5 billion) is about ten times the annual budget of UNHCR which has responsibility to deal with 10-15 million refugees throughout the world.[29] John Salt concludes that although the Dublin Convention of June 1990 between members of the European Community has produced some agreement on the initial handling of asylum claims, no real progress has been made on the substantive problem of harmonising entry criteria and subsequent rights to mobility within the Community. There is clear consensus, among officials at least, that new mechanisms should be created to deal with their plight. For example, SOPEMI (1990) refers to a common resolve now present among OECD governments to avoid the potential large influx of asylum seekers. At present, Germany takes the largest number (121,300 in 1989), followed by France (61,400) but rates of increase have been high in Austria, Sweden, Switzerland and Belgium. Widgren argues that the bulk of asylum-seeker migration is not related to new crises; that most come from countries with a long history of labour emigration. The danger is that the more the asylum institution degenerates into an inadequate and costly mechanism, the greater will be the risk of erosion of public support for genuine refugees.[30]

Of the 15 million or more *refugees* in the world today, about 12 million come under UNHCR mandate; 2.5 million Palestine refugees being excluded. To these should be added 14 million displaced persons who, because they live in their country of origin, receive neither protection nor much support from international organizations. While some refugee populations appear to have become permanent, openings towards political solutions have occurred recently in Afghanistan, Indochina, Central America and Namibia. It is therefore likely that millions of refugees may soon be able to return to their countries of origin.[31] Indeed, the large increase in Asian-born components of immigration to the traditional receivers has been due in large measure to their refugee intakes being followed by family reunion after the mid-1970s. Africa, however, remains the main domicile of refugees, two-thirds of them have having been displaced by natural disaster, drought, ecological problems, internal conflict and wars of liberation. Adepoju contends that African governments regard the problem as essentially an African one. Few African refugees have been given asylum in western countries, unlike refugees from Indochina.[32] In this regard, it is worth noting that 90 per cent of the 2.3 million refugees who entered the United States after 1945 had fled communist regimes; about one-third were Indochinese, one-third Cuban and one-third eastern European.[33]

REGIONAL PATTERNS

Relative to the world's present population, and to international migration during the nineteenth century, current flows are not large. Their salient feature is that direction is more global and composition more diverse. Receiving-governments have, in general, maintained control over intakes, utilizing numbers and composition to facilitate achievement of socio-economic objectives, although experiences in each region have varied according to the stages of demographic transition reached by constituent countries. The case for examining trends and prospects on a regional basis rests mainly on the proposition that each region has a reasonable degree of economic and demographic homogeneity. Linkages between regions have in large part been due to historical patterns of political and economic contact although, as already noted, these have changed considerably during the last 40 years.

EUROPE

Recent and present patterns of migration within, from and into Europe are more complex, and therefore more difficult to unravel, than patterns in any other region with the possible exception of Africa. Rapidly-changing demographic, economic and political conditions have led to changes in direction and composition so great that statistical systems, never the most enlightening, are unable to clarify either trends or their compositions.[34]

The 1960s and early 1970s was a period of huge guest-worker migration from Mediterranean countries to western and northern Europe. The typical "twinning" of sending/receiving-countries that emerged during that period was based largely upon specific recruitment policies, the consequences of which are reflected today in the ethnic compositions of major receiving-populations. From the mid-1970s, however, higher rates of economic growth in sending-regions saw not only a slowing of flows to the north, but also a significant return of workers to the South. The first oil crisis also contributed to declining annual average flows into the North; recruitment of regular migrant labour virtually ceased and clandestine and irregular employment emerged as a "real problem".[35]

It is generally acknowledged that, after the mid-1980s, several converging trends caused a turning-point in European migration. Just as the 1970s had seen two oil shocks and increasing inflation, the 1980s saw a gradual improvement in productivity, competetiveness and a revival of markets which brought western European economies back to a path of non-inflationary growth.[36] Salt shows not only that recruitment of foreign labour in western Europe began to recover (though not to earlier levels) but that several traditional emigration countries became countries of net immigration. Their rapidly-growing economies offered opportunities for migrants from the southern and eastern Mediterranean and beyond.[37] Significant political events and changes in eastern Europe also culminated in what he called the "mass moves of 1989-90" which led to the possibility of market-based migration within the eastern States as well as West-East migration of professional and technical workers to assist in the development of a unified European economy. The signing of the Single European Act has already focussed attention on the integration of European business, the Schengen Agreement is creating rules governing cross-border migration, and within the European Community a "ring fence" has been foreshadowed.

Table 1 (see p. 53), drawn from SOPEMI sources, shows the 1989 stock of foreign labour (not foreign population) in selected European OECD countries. France, Germany and the United Kingdom have the largest numbers, a legacy of long-standing and sustained policies to supplement their labour forces with workers from abroad. However, eastern Europe has become a major source of new immigrants. In 1989, 1.3 million entered western Europe - 80,000 asylum seekers (mainly from Poland and Yugoslavia), 150,000 Jews and others from the Soviet Union and 720,000 Germans, of whom 345,000 were from the former German Democratic Republic and the remainder from Poland and other eastern European countries.[38] Table 2 (see p. 54) shows that, in 1990, over 400,000 persons applied for asylum status in western European countries. In the regions's rapidly changing labour markets the asylum-seeker phenomenon is clearly testing the capacity of regulatory systems as well as the resolve of recipient countries.

While no one disputes that the asylum-seeker phenomenon, together with growing pressure through normal channels from the East, have become major migration issues in western Europe, changes in numbers and composition of achieved immigration to countries in southern Europe have been rapid and, to a large extent, unexpected . At the end of 1990, *Italy* was host to an estimated 80,000 Moroccans, 41,000 Tunisians, 34,000 Filipinos, 30,000 Yugoslavs and 25,000 Senegalese. In 1989, Spain had 400,000 foreign residents, double the number in 1980, two-thirds having come from other European countries, one-fifth from the Americas and 7 per cent from Africa and Asia. *Portugal* had an estimated 100,000 foreign nationals in 1989, mainly from Cape Verde, Brazil, the United Kingdom and Spain. Although estimates for *Greece* are not available, it is believed that recent intakes comprise many Pontions and Albanians as well as migrants from Ethiopia, Poland, Iran and the Middle East. There has also been a substantial increase in the number of "permanent" immigrants from the Maghreb, Poland, Turkey and parts of Asia to France, the Netherlands and, to a lesser extent, Belgium (SOPEMI, 1990, pp.10-12). Countries which in the recent past have supplied labour are now drawing large numbers of workers from the Third World and eastern Europe. Indeed, within eastern Europe itself, Hungary is receiving migrants from Romania, the Soviet Union and the Middle East.[39/]

There is no doubt that European migration is in a state of considerable flux. Chief among the causes stand high though variable rates of economic growth in EC countries; changing production techniques and composition of labour demand; greatly-reduced rates of population growth (by 2025, Europe's share of world population is expected to have declined from 1/10th to 1/20th); and major changes in political power and systems within the European Community as well in nearby regions.[40/] The European Community is a strong magnet not only for migrants from non-EC Europe, but also from such neighbouring regions as the Maghreb and other regions at early stages of demographic transition.

Despite these pressures, western European countries, by and large, have not readily acknowledged that they have become countries of immigration in the sense that, in addition to admitting foreign workers to plug labour gaps, they also admit immigrants and allow workers to achieve immigrant status. Indeed, Europe heads the OECD league in annual registered immigration. Since 1984/85, the annual average number of foreign residents permitted to settle in western European countries has been between 0.8 to 0.9 million compared with 0.6 to 0.7 million immigrants entering the United States, which is widely acknowledged as the world's major traditional receiver.[39/] In his recent survey of European migration policies, David Coleman showed that, in view of its large foreign-born population, the Netherlands has "become a *de facto* immigration country and will remain so...even though it has never sought that status". Likewise, Germany does not regard itself as a country of immigration even though, in 1988, 4.49 million foreigners, representing 7.5 per cent of the population, lived there.[41/]

High per capita incomes in the European Community have created, and will continue to create, pressures for entry from persons living in poorer countries (especially those in nearby southern and the eastern Mediterranean regions), former colonies now comprising the South, and especially eastern Europe and the Soviet Union where political turmoil and uncertainty has intensified. Demographic/economic pressure has been especially strong in southern Mediterranean countries where differential population growth rates of around 2 per cent relative to northern Mediterranean countries are expected to continue into the 1990s and could well cause some sending-countries actually to encourage their people to emigrate.[42/] Former colonial ties have always encouraged migration paths although, in the case of United Kingdom, these were effectively restricted by legislation in the early 1960s. However, the return of former emigrants to their European homelands represents a sustained addition to the populations of some countries. In the case of Portugal, for example, the 1981 census showed that the 505,000 persons who had returned from Africa (mainly from Angola and Mozambique) represented 5.1 per cent of Portugal's population.[43/] Return migration from the traditional receivers to European homelands was considerable after the early 1970s and can be expected to continue as many of the millions of Europeans who emigrated to the United States, Canada and Australia decided to return following their retirement from the respective workforces.

THE UNITED STATES, CANADA AND AUSTRALIA: TRADITIONAL RECEIVERS

Each of the traditional receivers has hardly wavered in its commitment to admit large numbers of immigrants for permanent settlement. Decisions taken by their governments concerning numbers and composition normally attract considerable public debate which, in turn, generally results in operational changes without compromising policy objectives. The institution of immigration in the traditional receivers, writes Papademetriou, is largely the result of a shared fundamental belief in its value in nation-building and as an important positive economic force. It also represents a commitment to family reunification and a "remarkably liberal response to refugees".[44/]

The United States takes by far the lion's share of the world's permanent immigrants and the western hemisphere is by far its main source. Table 3 (which includes almost half a million persons whose presence was legalised - see p. 55) shows that 63 per cent of immigrants in 1989 were from the western hemisphere compared with 28 per cent from Asia and only 9 per cent for Europe. This represents a major change in sources since the early 1960s. Although an overwhelming proportion of immigrants enter through the family-reunification system,[45/] 54,000 foreign nationals, equally distributed between "professional" and "skilled/unskilled" categories, entered on employment-based visas in 1989 because their services had been sought by US businesses.[46/] The United States Government estimates that despite recent legislation designed to regularize illegal migration, there may still be between two and three million illegals in the country and the annual inflow may be of the order of 200,000.[47/] The United States also issued 2.6 million temporary visas in 1989 for business, temporary work and training.

Canada's permanent immigration programme has similar objectives: reunification of close family members, to fulfil obligations to refugees and uphold the country's tradition in respect of displaced persons.[48/] In 1989, Canada admitted 190,342 immigrants - 91,998 from Asia,* 51,828 from Europe, 12,774 from North and Central America and 12,148 from Africa. In addition, the Government issued 284,788 employment authorizations. Its Business Immigration programme, designed to attract foreign business expertise, technology and investment issued 4,662 visas. Entrepreneurs and investors under that programme declared funds totalling Canadian $ 4.1 billion.[49/]

Australia, which has been very professional in its approach to immigration, in the sense that successive post-war governments have been committed to maintaining a programme for basically demographic (nation building) and economic reasons, has seen immigrants contribute 40 per cent of its population growth from 7 million (1945) to 17 million today. Family reunion, independent and refugee programmes are similar to those adopted by the United States and Canada. In the fiscal year 1989/90, 121,227 settlers were admitted to Australia, 40 per cent from Asia,** 31 per cent from Europe (19 per cent from the UK) and 14 per cent from Oceania (mainly New Zealand). As in the United States, family reunion is the main component; in 1990/1991, 64,000 persons will be admitted under that programme, 50,000 under the skill migration and 11,000 under humanitarian programmes. Similar to the United States and Canada, Australia has a temporary resident scheme; in 1989/90, visas were issued

---

* Including Hong Kong 20,001; the Philippines 11,363; Vietnam 8,470; India 8,804 and Lebanon 6,145.

** Hong Kong 11,538; Malaysia 8,073; Philippines 6,233; Viet Nam 4,691; China 3,894 and India 2,278.

to 106,000 foreigners, mainly "working holiday-makers" and specialist- and executive-class workers.[50]

Aside from similarity of policy objectives, the important feature (for purposes of this Monograph) of contemporary immigration to the traditional receivers is the increase, after the mid-1960s, in the number of source countries, most of which are in the South. However, the policies giving rise to these changes were not premised on resolution of South-North emigration pressure. Many settlers have in fact been professional and highly skilled who comprised the braindrain from developing countries. The bulk of subsequent migration has been through family reunion initiated by these migrants and by refugees who arrived under various humanitarian programmes. The entry of Mexicans to the United States in such large numbers (see Table 3, p. 55) represents the only example of substantial migration to a traditional receiver occurring outside the regulatory system that can be attributed to "emigration pressure".

SOUTH AMERICA AND THE CARIBBEAN

From being a major receiver of permanent immigrants from Europe until the 1950s, South America (and in particular Latin America) is now a minor receiver of settlers from other continents. Only Venezuela in the southern continent can now "boast of having an effective pro-immigration policy".[51] The prime reason, and there are others, has been low rates of economic growth associated with high rates of population growth. The region as a whole actually experienced negative rates of growth in per capita GDP between 1980-85 (-1.6%) and the trend is still downward. Though overall fertility rates are high, specific rates are lower in the high-income countries.*

As already noted, the region has become a major source of immigrants for the United States (Table 3). Mexico and Cuba have been the main providers and recent flows from the region have included an increasing number of females and dependants. Alfredo Lattes and Z.R. de Lattes calculate that sustained emigration has led to a stock of probably ten million Latin American and Caribbean migrants living outside the region.[52] In emphasising the braindrain dimensions of this migration, G. Clivaggio

---

* Argentina 2.9, Brazil 3.3, Chile 2.7, Colombia 3.0, Venezuela 3.6, Dominican Republic 3.5, Nicaragua 5.3, Bolivia 5.9, Guatemala 5.6. (UNDP, *Human Development Report 1991*, Oxford, 1991, Table 21, pp. 160-1).

estimates that approximately 50,000 Argentine scientists were "known to be living abroad" and, on the basis of the 1980 US Census, over 53 per cent of Colombians legally admitted to that country had more than twelve years schooling.[53/]

An important recent migration trend has been the flow to their ethnic 'homelands' of second and third-generation Europeans and Asians, presumably attracted by both higher income, stable employment and perhaps the warm welcome that immigrants of ethnic background different to the host country sometimes do not receive. SOPEMI (1990) reported that one-fifth of the legally-registered foreign residents in Spain came from the United States, Argentina, Venezuela, Chile and Cuba, and over 10 per cent of Portugal's foreign nationals were from Brazil. The Lattes report that Latin American descendants of Europeans are increasingly adopting the nationality of their ancestors as a way of acquiring the right to settle in European countries. "In Argentina, long waiting-lines at the door of the Italian Consulate to procure Italian nationality have been a common sight in the last several years".[54/] Concerning the return of ethnic Asians, it has been estimated that 40,000 to 50,000 South Americans of Japanese descent (mainly from Brazil) are presently employed in Japan's automobile and apparel industries.[55/]

Of importance equal to the loss of emigrants to other countries, has been intra-regional migration between countries experiencing differential rates of economic growth, per capita incomes and employment opportunities. Much of this migration has been from rural areas in low-income countries to urban areas in neighbouring higher-income countries. Consistent with the transition explanation, though requiring a lot more research to unravel, large numbers of migrant workers are moving from countries at low stages to countries at higher stages of modernization. For example, Argentina, Venezuela and Brazil, with real GDP per capita (1985-1988) of $4,360, $5,650 and $4,620 respectively have been the main receivers of migrants from nearby countries. Most of the migrants going to Argentina and Venezuela have been described as "poor peasants" from Paraguay ($2,590), Bolivia ($1,480), Chile ($4,720) and Colombia ($3,810)".[56/] An "intense migratory process" is also occurring of Uruguayans to Europe, North America and Australia concurrently with emigration to Brazil and Argentina as a result of political crisis. The Lattes estimate that 300,000 Uruguayans were living in foreign countries in 1980 (the country's 1985 population was only 3 million), but during the last few years a number of them have returned home as a consequence of "normalization of the national political institutions".

Although reliability of estimates must be questioned, there seems little doubt that the Lattes are correct in their evaluation that intra-regional migration in the southern Cone intensified in the 1970s. Migration, including intercontinental migration, is at present occurring at the "highest numbers ever observed".

EAST AND SOUTH EAST ASIA

Dominated demographically by the People's Republic of China, which has played a relatively minor role in recent international migration, this region (together with South Asia), has become the "... main source region of permanent emigrants, refugees and contract migrant labour to other parts of the world".[57/] The importance of the Philippines, Hong Kong and Malaysia as sources of permanent emigrants to the traditional receivers has already been noted. Former political (especially colonial) ties facilitated early post-war flows to parts of Europe, but after the mid-1960s, opportunities for emigration to Europe and the traditional receivers were restricted to persons who had the appropriate skills. Family reunification programmes also contributed substantially to later emigration.

Two unexpected events in the 1970s led to further emigration. Following the huge increase in oil prices in 1973, oil-producing countries in the Middle East with small populations sought large numbers of contract workers to service their high rates of economic growth. They were drawn from nearby non-oil-producing countries and from Asia where the impact of labour emigration has been described as the most prominent development in Asia since the mid-1970s. Between 1969 and 1989 an estimated 11.82 million Asians worked in other countries, mainly in the Middle East and in 1990 over three million were estimated to be working in that region.[58/] The Philippines, with a mid-1987 population of 58 million and gross national product (GNP) per capita of $590, was the main source of supply from East and Southeast Asia, followed by Thailand, Korea and Indonesia (see Table 4, p. 56 and 57). Among the main impacts of labour emigration on sending-countries have been the contribution of remittances to balance of payments, reduction of unemployment and acquisition of skills which some returnees utilized upon their return.[59/]

The second unexpected event to have an important emigration impact was the Vietnam conflict. In its aftermath, several western countries, especially the traditional receivers, offered permanent settlement to Indochinese refugees living in camps within countries of first asylum. As with other types of permanent emigration, these prime flows had significant secondary effects through reunification.

Until quite recently, intra-regional migration had been quite small but recent changes were due mainly to East and South East Asia becoming what Lin Lean Lim aptly describes as the most economically dynamic region in the contemporary world. Japan has been, without question, the initiator of this achievement. Its own economic recovery after World War II was no less a miracle than Germany's. However, unlike Germany, Japan preferred to meet labour shortages by encouraging capital intensive production at home and investing in nearby low labour-cost countries, thus avoiding the need to bring "guest workers" to Japan. Between the 1960s and 1980s, professional transients from Japan and elsewhere also played important roles in advising on the construction and operation of factories in low labour-cost countries. The income and employment multipliers from these investment and labour policies, together with global demand for the products, initiated very high rates of economic growth and rapid increases in GNP per capita in the receiving-countries which, in turn, were responsible for the "four dragons" (Hong Kong, Taiwan, Korea and Singapore) completing demographic transition in what Lin Lean Lim describes as record time. These trends placed unusual pressure on labour supply. Indeed, by the turn of the century, their demographic growth is expected to be less than 1 per cent a year. Population-ageing will therefore become an increasingly important issue for each of these countries.

Cleverly working back up their assembly chains as far as capital-goods production, the NICs are now significant investors in other countries in the region. Between 1986 and 1989, while Japan invested $11 billion in three other fast-growing Asian economies with a combined population of 250 million (Malaysia, Thailand and Indonesia), the "four dragons" invested an equal amount in the same countries. By contrast, the United States invested $3 billion.[60] As these countries reached higher levels of development, and found their comparative advantage affected by labour costs, they too have shifted *their* production to less technologically-advanced, labour-plentiful countries.[61] This pattern is, of course, entirely consistent with the transition model articulated earlier in this Monograph.

High but variable rates of economic growth and demographic transition in most countries comprising East and South East Asia have led to labour migration flows that would have been unthinkable a decade ago. The attraction of *permanent residence* in the traditional receivers is still strong amongst Malaysians, Filipinos and residents of Hong Kong which, collectively, may have lost 200,000 persons since 1984. The increasing propensity of Taiwanese to emigrate has been explained by *The Nation* of 8 October 1990 as due to three generations of economic development having created a "broad class of people with enough money to do what they want" (like going to Australia or Canada as business migrants). It is not a prospect that governments of countries in the region relish, simply because highly-skilled and professional workers and entrepreneurs are needed to sustain their high rates of economic growth. Taiwan, Singapore and Thailand have recently made various attempts to attract back highly skilled and professional nationals who emigrated some years ago.[62/]

Although the Middle East remains a major destination for *contract labour* from the region, especially from countries at early stages of transition, high rates of economic growth in Japan and the "four dragons" have made the countries attractive destinations for workers from other countries in the region (see Table 4). Having succumbed to contract labour as one means of alleviating its labour shortage, *Japan* (with an expected shortfall of 2.7 million workers by the end of the century) hosted 81,407 legal foreign workers (mostly entertainers, business executives and language teachers) in 1988. By mid-1990, there was also an estimated 300,000 illegal workers mainly in small industries and construction. They had come mostly from the Philippines, Bangladesh, Pakistan and China.[63/]

Of the "four dragons", *Singapore* has an estimated 120,000-150,000 foreign workers. Most are unskilled, but government policy encourages upgrading with the incentive of permanent status. The workers come mainly from countries at early stages of transition: Indonesia, Thailand, Sri Lanka, India and Bangladesh. There may also be many illegal workers in Singapore. A recent amnesty, which threatened severe action against those who did not come forward, saw 11,000 respond.[64/] *Hong Kong*, despite labour shortages, has been reluctant to admit contract workers, but following pressures placed on the Government by employers, intake was raised to 16,700 in May 1990. After 6 months, employers sought 57,000 workers, four times the annual quota. Demand of this kind has, of course, attracted many illegal migrants. In May 1988, 13,300 were apprehended, representing only the "tip of the iceberg". These trends should, however, be set against the loss of over 200,000 residents since 1984 mainly in response to Beijing's impending takeover of the Colony in 1997.[65/]

Taiwan, with an average annual growth in per capita income of about 14 per cent, has attracted about 200,000 illegal foreign workers (visitors who overstay) as well as 40,000 contract workers from the Philippines, Thailand and Indonesia, and many overseas Chinese from South East Asia.[66/] In 1983, there were 18,000 *Korean* workers in other Asian countries; by 1988, there were only 8,215. High rates of economic growth has led to a current net *immigration* of workers from other countries. Numbers are not available but, according to Charles W. Stahl, there has been a large inflow of illegal workers from low-wage countries in Asia to do those manual and dirty jobs avoided by Koreans. It appears that an effort is being made to "import unskilled workers from China", including ethnic Koreans from both China and the Soviet Union.[67/]

Elsewhere in the region, labour migration flows are equally diverse and multi-directional. *Brunei,* another small but wealthy state, employs 87,000 foreigners in its private sector. Among the traditional sending-countries, *Thailand* still provides thousands of workers to Brunei, Japan, Hong Kong and Singapore, but because of high demand for labour in low-paid jobs, is now accepting workers from lesser-developed Cambodia and Burma. Although *Indonesia* provided 292,000 workers to 31 countries between 1984 and 1989, the most significant outflow has been of illegal workers to *Malaysia*, described as epitomizing the "complex web of interconnected flows" that are now occurring in the region. Malaysia's illegal population of Indonesians could be one million, again drawn mainly to employment in plantations which upwardly-mobile Malaysians avoid. The largest legal flows are to Singapore where Malaysians account for 60 per cent of the foreign workforce. In the *Philippines,* most Asia-bound workers go to Japan (including an estimated 115,000 female domestics/entertainers), Hong Kong and Singapore. Labour emigration is an important, government-backed operation which, between 1985-1989, totalled 2.3 million persons. Perhaps more than any country in the region, the Philippines shows much less propensity to accept workers partly because the country's demographic transition stalled in the 1970s and political upheavals have exacerbated emigration-mindedness.

High economic growth and sustained investment had led to a significant increase in the number of *professional transients* to the region. According to Philip Martin, over 25,000 of the 150,000 foreign workers in Singapore in 1990 were skilled or professional and the Government had established a clear policy of attracting such persons as settlers.[68/] Capital-assisted migration to the other "dragons" as well as to Malaysia and Thailand has also increased. Lin Lean Lim is convinced that increased numbers have been necessary to manage capital flows and oversee multinational projects and that the ethnic composition of transients has changed with the composition of foreign investment.[69/]

Although the Indochinese *refugee* situation is nowhere near as intense as in the late 1970s, the number of refugees in the region remains large. Table 5 (see p. 58) shows that, in 1989, Vietnamese refugees in other countries numbered 57,000 in Hong Kong, 21,700 in Malaysia, 26,100 in the Philippines, 16,900 in Thailand and 5,100 in Indonesia. However, by far the largest population of refugees consisted of 320,900 Cambodians and 77,700 Laotians in Thailand. Although these numbers represent the aftermath of a conflict long since formally over, the problems for nearly half a million people remain largely unresolved.

THE MIDDLE EAST

The main recent migration flows in this region have been millions of contract workers to oil-producing states from both Asia and nearby Arab non-oil-producing countries after 1973; permanent emigration from Arab states to the traditional receivers; and the settlement in Israel of Jewish people from many parts of the world.

The arrival of contract workers in the region did not begin with the oil crisis. The Gulf region has a long history of receiving workers from outside the region, in particular from the Indian sub-continent, as well as intra-Gulf migration prior to World War II.[70/] In 1973, the total population of the Gulf Cooperation Council (GCC) States (Saudi Arabia, Oman, Kuwait, Bahrain, UAE and Qatar) was less than 6 million, of whom about 4.5 million lived in Saudi Arabia. The oil boom created an enormous demand for labour in these countries, especially for semi- and unskilled labour on construction projects. Of the migrant labour in GCC States in 1975, 35 per cent were employed in the construction and 29 per cent in the service sectors. In the United Arab Emirates, 84 per cent of the total workforce was expatriate, and in Saudi Arabia, the figure was 40 percent.[71/] The 1.3 million workers from other Arab states in 1975 represented about 70 per cent of the expatriate workforce, four out of five being Egyptians and Palestinians/Jordanians. However, by the early 1980s, labour flows from other Arab states had slowed; Jordan and Yemen actually experiencing net return.[72/] Indeed, two-way migration has become a characteristic of the region. Oman, for example, was employing 70,000 expatriates in 1975 while 38,400 of its nationals were working in Saudi Arabia and the United Arab Emirates.

The importance of Asia as a source of labour increased enormously after 1975 when an estimated 360,000 workers represented 20 per cent of the region's non-national workforce. By 1985, there were about 3.5 million. Table 4 shows that between 1976 and 1989 intakes from both South East Asia (in particular, the Philippines and Thailand) and South Asia (in particular, Bangladesh, India and Pakistan) were sustained, although relative shares from each region have changed. In 1975, India and Pakistan accounted for 95 per cent of Asian workers in the Middle East; by 1989 their share was probably less than 25 per cent, South East and East Asia having become the main regions of supply.

Changes in ethnic composition have been accompanied by changes in skill composition. By 1987, services, manufacturing, public utilities and agriculture had become the main labour-short sectors, which led to a marked increase in the number of female workers from Sri Lanka, Bangladesh and Indonesia. For example, the number of female domestics from Indonesia increased from 8,000 in 1979 to over 50,000 in 1989.

The Gulf crisis of late 1990 not only saw the departure of hundreds of thousands of Arab and Asian workers from the Gulf, but cast doubts over near-future supplies from several sources. Prior to the crisis, Jordanians and Palestinians came from the West Bank across borders with Kuwait and other Gulf states whereas Asians had to rely on more formal avenues for their entry. Following political alignments during the crisis, there is likely to be a change in the ethnic make-up of labour and skill composition.

Although there has been a sustained flow of *permanent emigrants* from the region for several decades, numbers entering the traditional receiving countries have been small relative to numbers entering from Asia. Table 6 (see p. 59) not only shows that Iran has been the region's main supplier of immigrants to the United States since 1979 (followed by Lebanon, Jordan and Egypt) but that intakes from all countries in the region have remained unusually stable. For *Canada,* only Lebanon was listed among the top 20 "providers" of immigrants in 1988/89 (6,179). Other countries in the Middle East to supply more than one thousand immigrants in the same year were: Iran 3,797, Israel 1,740, Kuwait 1,414, Saudi Arabia 1,395, United Arab Emirates 1,172 and Syria 1,111. The stock of Middle East-born persons in *Australia* in the 1986 census was dominated by Lebanon (56,337), followed by Iran (7,497), Israel (7,003), Iraq (4,516) and Syria (3,863). Lebanon's prominence as a provider of Middle Eastern immigrants to both Canada and Australia reflects each country's willingness to make special arrangements for some Lebanese who had been displaced by prolonged warfare in their country. Family reunification has also contributed to the stocks of Lebanese in each of the traditional receivers. Prolonged warfare also largely explains why 9,300 Lebanese sought asylum in European and North American countries in 1988 and 15,700 in 1989.[73/]

As shown in Table 7 (see p. 60), Israel has been a destination for Jewish people from all over the world. An estimated 482,000 immigrants arrived between 1919 and the birth of the State of Israel in 1948, of which 377,000 were from Europe. Since then, the main regions of supply have been Europe (especially Poland and Romania in the early post-war years, and the Soviet Union since 1989), Asia (especially Iraq and Iran in the 1950s and 1960s) and North Africa (especially Morocco and Tunisia in the 1950s and 1960s and Ethiopia since 1980). The Soviet Union is the last major reservoir of Jewish people available (and likely) to settle in Israel. Recent major political changes in the Soviet Union have increased the prospects for an estimated 2 million Soviet Jews to emigrate to Israel.[74/]

SOUTH ASIA

Three distinct phases of emigration from the Asian sub-continent (India, Pakistan, Bangladesh and Sri Lanka) can be identified after 1834. The first (1834-1937), saw over 30 million persons emigrate as indentured workers to plantations in countries bordering the Indian Ocean and the Caribbean.[75/] The second phase occurred after the Second World War when thousands of unskilled and semi-skilled workers settled in the United Kingdom; and after the late 1960s when the traditional receivers favoured the admission of professional and skilled workers. Also after World War II, the partition of India and Pakistan caused about seven million Hindus to move from Pakistan to India and an approximately equal number of Muslims to move from India to Pakistan. The third phase began in the 1970s with labour migration to the Middle East (Table 4).

The region has a low per capita income, slow economic growth and accounts for over half the world's poorest people. Had more opportunities for emigration been available, there is little doubt that many more persons would have left the sub-continent. The recent decline in labour migration has been caused mainly by a shift in demand towards professional and highly-skilled workers although a large number of such workers have already replaced westerners and non-national Arabs in the Middle East because they are prepared to work for lower wages.[76/] Pakistan and India provided 27 per cent and Bangladesh and Sri Lanka 22 per cent of the estimated 795,900 workers in the Middle East in 1989. The economic impact of sustained labour emigration, especially through remittance payments, has been considerable.[77/]

With the rapid expansion of labour markets in East Asia during the last few years, and the changing composition of labour demand in the Middle East, one would have expected South Asia to become a more important source of labour for East Asia than shown in Table 4. Instead, East Asia's labour demand has been met mainly by workers from within the region, especially Filipinos and Thais. The toe-holds achieved in Japan and the "four dragons" by South Asians have been by small numbers of legal and illegal workers. Indeed, Pakistanis topped the list of illegal workers detained in Japan in 1989; and in 1990 Bangladeshis won that prize.[78/] Although proximity partly explains why Filipinos and Thais have succeeded in obtaining the largest shares of jobs held by foreigners, aggressive promotion by their governments and agents have also contributed.

The closing of entry to unskilled workers by many countries and deteriorating economic conditions have clearly exacerbated emigration pressure in parts of South Asia, especially in Bangladesh. It has the lowest per capita income of all the South Asian countries, extreme poverty is widespread and there is a chronic balance-of-payments deficit. India, on the other hand, with a large industrial sector, stands a better chance of providing the type of workers increasingly demanded in Middle East and East Asia. The recent increased demand for female domestic workers in both these regions has been met mainly by Sri Lanka. A recent Colombo airport survey showed that 65 per cent of "worker departures" were females.[79/]

One of the lesser-known migration flows occurs between South Asian countries. Data are sparse, but it appears that a considerable exchange of labour occurs across the relatively open borders between India and Bangladesh, and India and Nepal. Migration is occuring between Bangladesh and Pakistan, via India, and although most of the migrants have settled in Karachi, reliable estimates of numbers are not available. Table 5 on refugee populations in Asia is dominated by the 3.62 million Afghans in Pakistan. Many are already integrated into the Pakistani labour market and apparently do not want to be repatriated. According to Lin Lean Lim, they are "principally economic rather than political refugees". Table 5 also shows that India hosts 100,000 refugees from China (Tibet), 91,500 from Sri Lanka and 96,000 from Bangladesh.

SUB-SAHARAN AFRICA

On 29 August 1991, the Secretary-General of the United Nations, Javier Pérez de Cuellar wrote that Africa will sink deeper into an "unrelenting crisis of tragic proportions" unless world leaders agree to cancel its debts and substantially increase international efforts to revive its economy. The situation in Africa, he reported, represented the "greatest development challenge of our time" and only a worldwide effort aimed at the structural transformation of African economies could eliminate the poverty which grips most of the continent's people.[80/]

The magnitude of sub-Saharan Africa's poverty is verified by available data. The *Human Development Report for 1991* showed that for *every* index of human development (including GNP/capita, life expectancy, maternal mortality, adult literacy and annual population growth) sub-Saharan Africa was below the world average and on some items was the world's worst. Economic growth has been slow, GNP per capita has been falling by an average 2.2 per cent a year during the last ten years, an estimated 100 million persons are unemployed and possibly an equal number are underemployed. Rapid growth in population combined with stagnant economic growth has been a major reason for the continent's poverty and unemployment.

Following his assessment of appropriate statistics, Adepoju concluded that Africa has experienced a devastating socio-economic crisis during the last decade. It now contains two-thirds of the world's least-developed countries. In the 1980s, 20 African countries experienced negative growth rates. Sixteen per cent of the world's poorest people live there, an estimate that is projected to increase to 32 per cent by the end of the century. Deterioration in the terms of trade of most countries derives mainly from falling commodity prices and rising import prices. Overall economic conditions have been worsened by the debt burden which doubled between 1980 and 1986.[81/]

Uneven distribution of resources and employment opportunities between the large number of countries in sub-Saharan Africa has led to substantial migration of all types. Although there has not been a comprehensive review of international migration in the region for some time, recent monographs by Russell, Jordan and Stanley, and by Sergio Ricca convey overviews of general trends.[82/] Sharon S. Russell, *et al.*, conclude that because data on migration flows in the region are virtually non-existent, reliance has to be placed on data relating to stocks of foreigners in each country. From these data, they calculate that as the proportion of total immigrants in the region's 433 million population (1983) is 3.08 per cent, the number of immigrants could be 13.4 million. "If one then makes the heroic assumption that refugees are not counted in census data", and adds the UNHCR estimate of 3.9 million for 1988, the total population of international migrants is in the range of 17.3 million. And if one further adds "persons in refugee-like circumstances living outside their countries of origin", the overall estimate of 35 million calculated by Ricca is plausible. This represented 8 per cent of sub-Saharan Africa's population in 1983. Ricca's estimate had included Africans and persons from other continents who had crossed one or more international borders between their country of origin and their country of residence*. Of course, the data bases used to reach these estimates vary enormously in both quality and age.

Migration, wrote Ricca, has been part of the African way of life for generations; trader and pastoral nomadism being a distinguishing cultural feature of many African populations. The need for water and grazing land, barter and trade, conquest and response to natural disaster contributed to migration flows in pre-colonial times. The main effect of colonial conquest, he notes, was to "move the centre of gravity of economic activity from the inland savannahs to the coastal areas of the rain forests and to create centres of development on the sites of the continent's main mineral deposits". New crops introduced by Europeans saw large areas of land being taken

---

* Sergio Ricca (pp. 58-9) presents a useful analysis of "where legality ends and clandestinity begins" in relation to migration in Africa.

over for plantations. These changes, together with the slave trade, led inevitably to large-scale redistribution of Africa's population.[83/]

The observation that present-day migration flows appear to have been caused mainly by migrant labour moving from rural areas to urban centres, especially to areas of higher development (and investment), led Ricca to conclude that the economic factor had come to dominate migration and that the "cultural element characteristic of migration in pre-colonial Africa is gradually disappearing". While Figure 3 (see p. 61) shows the principal migratory flows in Africa during the 1980s, compositions and their causes are very difficult to assess. For example, in *East Africa,* which has a long history of intra-continental labour migration, there has been substantial migration from Sudan to the Middle East. However, overall migration has been dominated by refugees, not just in the Horn, but also in the southern countries of East Africa. Russell, *et al.,* show that Mozambique now accounts for 29 per cent of the region's refugees and that Malawi, Zambia and Zimbabwe rank among the top ten asylum countries. Migration in *Central Africa,* on the other hand, is characterised by a variety of types, *West Africa* by the highest concentration of migrants and *Southern Africa* by flows determined largely by employment opportunities in the Republic of South Africa (Figure 3).

These broad generalisations hide many smaller streams of different compositions (including type and feminisation) caused by both economic opportunity, warfare and political strife. While the overwhelming proportion of sub-Saharan migration is intra-continental, there is some migration, especially permanent and of asylum seekers to other regions. Refugees have not been dispersed to Europe or the traditional receivers in the manner of Indochinese refugees, and the figures on recent permanent migration to the traditional receivers shows that Africa is only a minor source. However, Russell, *et al.,* conclude that a substantial number of highly-trained Africans live abroad and their exodus has created shortages and bottlenecks in some sending-countries. A new, probably more serious problem is that many recent graduates have been unable to obtain jobs in Africa or to emigrate. This has shifted the problem from "overall shortage to one of poor distribution and limited opportunities".[84/] Adepoju has also noted this problem; unemployment, he concludes, is "fast creeping up the educational ladder". A recent survey in Côte d'Ivoire showed that 37 per cent of persons holding university degrees in Abidjan were unemployed, and the quality of education was suffering from reduced university funding. This means not only that few qualified Africans are able to secure places in African universities, but that opportunities to emigrate abroad are being adversely affected by declining standards of education.

Although Mahgreb countries provide a high proportion of current immigrant workers in southern Europe, significant numbers are also provided by Eritrea, Somalia, Gambia, Ghana and Guinea; most are there illegally and experience high rates of unemployment. At the end of 1989, an estimated 15,000 Mozambicans were in (what was then) East Germany.[85/]

Labour migration (legal and illegal) *within* sub-Saharan Africa simply cannot be adequately assessed even though it is a feature of all sub-regions. Based on census data of variable quality and age, the proportions of immigrants in each country varied from 0.01 per cent in Madagascar (1975) to 21.5 per cent in Côte d'Ivoire. Russell's estimates show that proportions vary considerably, being highest in the 11 West African countries (approximately 6%) but only 2.5 per cent in the 16 East African countries. These differences are due mainly to levels of investment and economic development. In southern Africa, the Republic is a magnet to workers from neighbouring countries; during the 1980s, Lesotho, Mozambique and Malawi were the main providers, although flows have slowed, especially from Mozambique following internal military strife and the suspension of recruitment by South Africa. In West Africa, which has the highest concentration of immigrants, Nigeria was the main destination for migrants from Ghana, Togo, Benin, Niger and Chad during the 1970s (Figure 3). By 1982, it hosted an estimated 2.5 million non-nationals, but subsequent economic and political events combined to reduce flows substantially. Most of the migrants are thought to be young, male and generally illiterate; recent flows have included a higher proportion of women and children.

These examples merely illustrate what appear to be the main global stocks and flows. The whole migration situation is far too complex, and data too sparse, to provide anything more. As Papademetriou concludes, the worldwide widening and the deepening of the migration process is at its most complex and bewildering in Africa, rendering distinctions between internal and international flows "useless." With rapidly increasing populations, and demonstrably declining wealth, relative to the countries of the North, sub-Saharan Africa and South Asia are the two regions where present and potential emigration pressures are clearly the strongest.

NOTES

1. Demetrios G. Papademetriou, "International Migration in North America and Western Europe: Trends and Consequences", *International Migration Today,* Vol. 1, Trends and Prospects, UNESCO, Paris, 1988, p. 311.

2. Jonas Widgren, OECD paper, 1991, p. 1.

3. Statement by the Director General of IOM to the Round Table on the Movement of People: New Developments (mimeo), San Remo, 3-5 May 1990, pp. 5-7.

4. R. T. Appleyard, "Migration and Development: a critical Relationship", *Asian and Pacific Migration Journal,* Vol. 1, No. 1, (forthcoming).

5. Jonas Widgren, OECD paper, 1991, p. 4.

6. Aristide R. Zolberg, Astri Suhrke and Sergio Aguayo, *Escape from Violence. Conflict and the Refugee Crisis in the Developing World,* Oxford University Press, New York, 1989.

7. R. T. Appleyard, op.cit.; also, "International Migration and Development. Mauritius and Seychelles", a chapter in R. T. Appleyard and R. N. Ghosh (Editors), *Economic Planning and Performance in Indian Ocean Island States,* ANU, Canberra, 1990, pp.141-52.

8. ILO, Press. Regional Feature Service, (mimeo), nd., p. 1.

9. Quoted by David Turnham and Denizhan Eröcal, "The Supply of Labour, Employment Structures and Unemployment in Developing Countries", a paper presented at the OECD International Conference on Migration, Rome, March 1991, p. 5.

10. Jonas Widgren, *International Affairs* article, 1990, p. 753.

11. Director General of IOM, *International Migration*, Vol. XXIX, No. 2, June 1991, p. 160.

12. Jonas Widgren, *International Affairs* article, 1990, p. 756.

13. H. Zlotnik, op. cit., pp. 319-20 and Table 2.

14. Demetrios G. Papademetriou, OECD Rome paper 1991, p. 12.

15. J. N. Sarmiento, "The Asian Experience in International Migration", *International Migration,* Vol. XXIX, No. 2, June 1991, p. 200.

16. Reginald T. Appleyard, "General Introduction", *International Migration Today*, Vol. 1, Trends and Prospects, UNESCO, Paris, 1988, p. 11.

17. A. Adepoju, "South-North Migration: The African Experience", *International Migration,* Vol. XXIX, No. 2, June 1991, p. 211.

18. Jonas Widgren, *International Affairs* article, 1990, p. 755.

19. Paul J. Bailey and Aurelio Parisotto, "Multinational Enterprises: What Role can they play in Employment Generation in Developing Countries?", a paper presented at the OECD International Conference on Migration, Rome, March 1991, pp. 3-4.

20.
John Salt and Allan Findlay, "International Migration of Highly-Skilled Manpower: Theoretical and Developmental Issues", a chapter in Reginald Appleyard (Editor), *The Impact of International Migration on Developing Countries,* OECD, Paris, 1989.
21.
Demetrios G. Papademetriou, op. cit., p. 11.
22.
Alfredo Lattes and Z. R. Lattes, "International Migration in Latin America: Patterns, Implications and Policies", a paper presented at the UNFPA/ECE Informal Expert Group Meeting, Geneva, July 16-19, 1991, p. 6.
23.
John Salt, "Current and Future International Migration Trends Affecting Europe", a paper for the Fourth Conference of European Ministers responsible for Migration Affairs, Strasbourg, 1991, p. 13.
24.
SOPEMI Report, 1990, p. 1.
25.
Pietro Calamia, "The Outlook for Foreign Manpower in the Framework of the New Italian", a paper presented at the OECD International Conference on Migration, Rome, March 1991, p. 3.
26.
Anton Kuijsten, "International Migration in Europe: Patterns and Implications for Receiving Countries", a paper presented at the UNFPA/ECE Informal Expert Group Meeting, Geneva, July 16-19, 1991, p. 11.
27.
Jean-Claude Chesnais, "Soviet Emigration: Past, Present and Future", a paper presented at the OECD International Conference on Migration, Rome, March 1991, p. 3.
28.
John Salt, op. cit., Table 14.
29.
Demetrios G. Papademetriou, op. cit., p. 3.
30.
Jonas Widgren, OECD paper, 1991 p. 9.
31.
R. T. Appleyard, "Trends in International Migration in the 1990s", a paper presented to a seminar organized by the Centro di Studi Americani on Migration Policies in Europe and the United States, Rome, June 1991.
32.
Aderanti Adepoju, op. cit., p. 209.
33.
Demetrios G. Papademetriou, op. cit., p. 25.
34.
Anton Kuijsten, op. cit., pp. 1-4.
35.
IOM, "Migratory Movements from Central and East European Countries to Western Europe - some selected aspects", a document submitted to the Council of Europe Conference of Ministers on the Movement of persons coming from Central and Eastern European countries, Council of Europe, MMP (91) 4, Strasbourg, 1991, p. 1.
36.
Juhani Lönnroth, "Labour Market Policies for the 1990s", a paper presented at the OECD International Conference on Migration, Rome, March 1991, p. 4.
37.
John Salt, op. cit., p. 3.
38.
V. Grecic, "East-West Migration and its possible Influence on South-North Migration", *International Migration,* Vol. XXIX, No. 2, June 1991, p. 243.

39.

Jean-Claude Chesnais, op. cit., p. 3; Heinz Werner, "Migration Movements in the Perspective of the Single European Market", a paper presented at the OECD International Conference on Migration, Rome, March 1991, pp. 7-8.

40.

Jonas Widgren, ***International Affairs*** article, 1990, p. 453.

41.

David Coleman, "International Migrants in Europe: Adjustment and Integration Processes and Policies", a paper presented at the UNFPA/ECE Expert Group Meeting on International Migration, Geneva, 16-19 July 1991, pp. 10-19.

42.

Michele Bruni and Alessandra Venturini, "The Mediterranean Basin: Human Resources and Human Development", a paper presented at the OECD International Conference on Migration, Rome, March 1991, pp. 4-5.

43.

Americo Ramos dos Santos, "Return Migration of Portuguese from Africa and its Impact on the Portuguese Labour Market", a paper presented at the OECD International Conference on Migration, Rome, March 1991, p. 4.

44.

Demetrios Papademetriou, "International Migration in North America: Issues, Policies and Implications", a paper presented at the UNFPA/ECE Expert Group Meeting on International Migration, Geneva, 16-19 July 1991, p. 3.

45.

Ibid., p. 12.

46.

D. G. Papademetriou, "South-North Migration in the Western Hemisphere and U.S. Responses", ***International Migration,*** Vol. XXIX, No. 2, June 1991, p. 293.

47.

D. G. Papademetriou, *et al.,* The Effects of Employer Sanctions on the U.S. Labor Market, U.S. Department of Labor, International Labor Affairs Bureau, 1991.

48.

Mildred J. Morton, "Immigration to Canada: Policies of the 1980s. The Immigration Plan 1991-1995", Background Paper, IOM Ninth Seminar on South-North Migration, Geneva, December 1990.

49.

Employment and Immigration Canada, Annual Report, 1989-90, pp. 37 & 47.

50.

Australia, Bureau of Immigration Research, Immigration Update, December quarter, 1990, Table 1.10; Australia, "The Programming of Immigration Flows to Australia", Background Paper for the OECD International Conference on Migration, Rome, March 1991, p. 3.

51.

Jorge Balan, "Demographic Trends and Migratory Movements from Latin America and the Caribbean", a paper presented at the OECD International Conference on Migration, Rome, March 1991, p. 3.

52.

Alfredo Lattes and Z. R. de Lattes, op. cit., p. 7.

53.

C. M. Muñiz, "The Emigration of Argentine Professionals and Scientists", ***International Migration,*** Vol. XXIX, No. 2, June 1991, p. 232; R. Escobar-Navia, "South-North Migration in the Western Hemisphere", ***International Migration***, Vol. XXIX, No. 2, June 1991, p. 226.

54.

Alfredo Lattes and Z. R. de Lattes, op. cit., pp. 6-7.

55.

Philip L. Martin "Labor Migration in Asia", ***International Migration Review,*** Vol. 25, Spring 1991, p. 178.

56.
Alfredo Lattes and Z. R. de Lattes, op. cit., p. 14; UNDP *Human Development Report 1991*, Table 1.
57.
Lin Lean Lim, "The Demographic Situation and Migratory Movements in Asian Countries", a paper presented at the OECD International Conference on Migration, Rome, March 1991, p. 3.
58.
J. N. Sarmiento, "The Asian Experience in International Migration", *International Migration*, Vol. XXIX, No. 2, June 1991, p.197; Lin Lean Lim, op. cit., p. 5; C. W. Stahl, "South-North Migration in the Asia-Pacific Region", *International Migration*, Vol. XXIX, No. 2, June 1991, p.163; Philip Martin, op. cit., p.190.
59.
R.T. Appleyard, "Migration and Development: Myths and Reality", *International Migration Review*, Vol. 23, Fall 1989, pp. 486-99.
60.
C. W. Stahl, op. cit., p. 174; Philip Martin, op. cit., p. 177.
61.
Lin Lean Lim, "International Labour Migration in Asia: Patterns, Implications and Policies", a paper presented at the UNFPA/ECE Expert Group Meeting on International Migration, Geneva, July 1991, pp. 25 & 49.
62.
Lin Lean Lim, Rome paper, p. 20; Geneva paper, p. 15.
63.
C. W. Stahl, op. cit., p.168; Philip Martin, op. cit., p. 178.
64.
Philip Martin, op. cit., p.183; C. W. Stahl, op. cit., p.172; Lin Lean Lim, Geneva paper, pp. 12-3.
65.
Philip Martin, op. cit., pp.184-5; C. W. Stahl, op. cit., p.169; Lin Lean Lim, Rome paper, pp. 9-10.
66.
Lin Lean Lim, Geneva paper, p. 11; Rome paper, pp. 10-11.
67.
C. W. Stahl, op. cit., pp.165 & 173; Philip Martin, op. cit., p. 188; Lin Lean Lim, Geneva paper, p. 12.
68.
C. W. Stahl, op. cit., pp. 166, 168 & 170; Philip Martin, op. cit., p. 187; Lin Lean Lim, Rome paper, pp.15-16.
69.
C. W. Stahl, op. cit., p. 163; Philip Martin, op. cit., p. 182; Lin Lean Lim, Rome paper, p. 6.
70.
Ian J. Seccombe, "International Migration in the Middle East: Historical Trends, Contemporary Patterns and Consequences", *International Migration Today*, Vol. 1, Trends and Prospects, UNESCO, Paris, 1988.
71.
J. S. Birks and C. A. Sinclair, *International Migration and Development in the Arab Region*, ILO, Geneva, 1980; A. Kubursi, *The Economics of the Arabian Gulf. A Statistical Sourcebook*.
72.
A. Findlay, "The Role of International Labour Migration in the Transformation of an Economy. The case of the Yemen Arab Republic", ILO Working Paper, Geneva, 1987.
73.
Jonas Widgren, OECD paper, 1991, Table 3.
74.
R. T. Appleyard, "Trends in International Migration in the 1990s", a paper presented at the Centro di Studi Americani International Seminar, Rome, June 1991.
75.
K. Davis, *The Population of India and Pakistan*, Princeton, N. J., 1951, p. 99.

76.
Lin Lean Lim, Geneva paper, p. 17.
77.
N. Choucri, The Hidden Economy: A new View of Remittances in the Arab World, mimeo, MIT, Cambridge 1985; Manolo Abella, "International Migration in the Middle East: patterns and implications for sending countries", a paper delivered at the UNECE/UNFPA Informal Expert Group Meeting on International Migration, Geneva, 16-19 July 1991, pp. 37-8.
78.
R. T. Appleyard, "South Asia and the Indian Ocean", a paper presented to the Conference on International Manpower Flows and Foreign Investment in the Asian Region, Nihon University, Tokyo, September 9-12, 1991, pp. 7 & 11.
79.
Ibid., p. 11.
80.
The Times, 29 August 1991.
81.
Aderanti Adepoju, "South-North Migration: The African Experience", ***International Migration,*** Vol. XXIX, No. 2, June 1991, pp. 207-8.
82.
Sharon Stanton Russell, Karen Jacobsen and William Deane Stanley, ***International Migration and Development in sub-Sahara Africa,*** Vol. 1, Overview, World Bank Discussion Papers, Africa Technical Dept. Series, Washington, D. C., 1990; Sergio Ricca, op. cit.
83.
S. Ricca, op. cit., pp. 10-11.
84.
S.S. Russell, *et al.,* p. 6.
85.
SOPEMI, 1990, pp. 8-10; J. Salt, op. cit., p. 17.

TABLE 1

AVAILABLE INFORMATION ON STOCKS OF FOREIGN LABOUR IN SELECTED OECD COUNTRIES, 1980-1989
(thousands)

	1980	1981	1982	1983	1984	1985	1986	1987	1988	1989
Austria	178.4	177.9	166.2	154.8	146.7	148.3	155.0	157.7	160.9	178.0
Belgium	332.7	332.2	338.9	375.0	388.3	396.3	403.1	411.5	–	–
France	1 458.2	1 427.1	1 503.0	1 557.5	1 658.2	1 649.2	1 555.7	1 524.9	1 557.0	1 593.8
Germany	2 115.7	2 096.3	2 029.0	1 983.5	1 854.9	1 823.4	1 833.7	1 865.5	1 910.6	1 940.6
Luxembourg	51.9	52.2	52.3	53.8	53.0	–	–	–	–	–
Netherlands	188.1	192.7	185.2	173.7	168.8	165.8	169.0	175.7	176.0	192.0
Sweden	234.1	233.5	227.7	221.6	219.2	216.1	214.9	214.9	220.2	237.0
Switzerland (a)	501.2	515.1	526.2	529.8	539.3	549.3	566.9	587.7	607.8	631.8
United Kingdom	–	–	–	–	744.0	808.0	815.0	814.0	870.0	960.0

a) Seasonal and frontier workers are not taken into account.
Sources: SOPEMI: John Salt, "Current and Future International Migration Trends Affecting Europe", (mimeo), Strasbourg, 1991.

TABLE 2

APPLICATIONS FOR ASYLUM IN EUROPEAN COUNTRIES, 1980-1990

	1980	1981	1982	1983	1984	1985	1986	1987	1988	1989	1990*
Austria	9.3	34.5	6.3	5.9	7.2	6.7	8.7	11.4	15.8	22.8	25.0
Belgium	2.7	2.4	2.9	3.4	3.4	5.3	7.7	6.0	5.1	8.0	13.0
Denmark	–	–	–	0.8	4.3	8.7	9.3	2.1	4.7	4.6	5.5
France	13.7	9.2	12.6	14.3	15.9	25.8	23.4	24.8	31.6	60.0	52.0
Germany	107.8	49.4	37.2	19.7	35.3	73.9	99.7	57.4	103.1	121.0	200.0
Greece	1.8	2.3	1.2	0.5	0.8	1.4	4.3	7.0	–	–	–
Italy	2.5	3.6	3.2	3.1	4.6	5.4	6.5	10.9	–	–	–
Netherlands	3.2	1.6	1.8	2.0	2.6	5.7	5.9	14.0	7.5	14.0	19.0
Norway	–	–	–	0.2	0.3	0.9	2.7	8.6	6.6	4.4	4.0
Portugal	–	–	–	1.5	0.4	0.1	0.3	0.2	–	–	–
Spain	–	–	2.5	1.4	1.1	2.4	2.3	2.5	–	–	–
Sweden	–	–	–	3.0	12.0	14.5	14.6	18.5	19.6	32.0	32.0
Switzerland	6.1	5.2	7.2	7.9	7.5	9.7	8.6	10.9	16.7	24.5	35.0
United Kingdom	10.0	2.9	3.6	5.5	3.3	5.5	3.9	4.2	5.1	10.0	16.0
TOTAL	157.1	111.1	78.5	68.7	98.7	166.0	197.9	178.5	215.8	301.3	401.5

Source: OECD (1990); John Salt, "Current and Future International Migration Trends Affecting Europe", (mimeo), Strasbourg, 1991.
Note: * Provisional Data.

TABLE 3

IMMIGRATION TO THE UNITED STATES: 1989
(SELECTED COUNTRY OF LAST RESIDENCE)

Western Hemisphere			672,639
	Mexico	405,660	
	Central America	101,273	
	South America	59,812	
	Other	105,894	
Asia			296,420
	Philippines	66,119	
	Korea	33,016	
	India	28,599	
	China	39,284	
	Hong Kong	15,257	
	Viet Nam	13,174	
	Other	100,971	
Europe			94,338
	United Kingdom	16,961	
	Germany	10,419	
	Italy	11,089	
	Portugal	3,861	
	Other	52,008	
			1,063,397

Source: INS Statistical Yearbook 1989; Demetrios Papademetriou, (UNFPA/ECE paper) p. 13A, Figure 1), considers the figures an overview "... heavily 'contaminated' by partial data ...".

TABLE 4

REGIONAL DISTRIBUTION OF ASIAN LABOUR MIGRANTS
1976 - 1989

Sending Country Receiving Region	1976-79	1980	1981	1982	1983	1984	1985	1986	1987	1988	1989
Rep. of Korea											
Middle East	261 505*	120 535	138 310	151 583	130 776	100 765	72 907	44 753	31 069	21 542	
Asia	17 985*	4 095	9 178	12 597	18 092	16 350	5 590	4 882	6 813	8 215	
America	7 913*	154	70	857	1 853	805	1 418	2 093	2 659	1 894	
Europe	20 140*	3		288	5 360	378	320	338	742	646	
Africa	25 287*			278	555	308	795	458	757	455	
Seamen	111 832*	21 649	27 556	31 252	31 192	34 067	39 215	42 751	44 300	50 230	
TOTAL	444 662*	146 436	175 114	196 855	184 277	152 673	120 245	95 275	86 340	82 982	
Indonesia											
Middle East	7 651	11 501	11 484	9 595	17 899	28 702	48 280	42 144	48 834	53 208	
Asia	884	1 227	2 544	8 440	5 890	6 942	5 930	21 253	7 984	6 485	
America			50	1 085	1 948	686	985		1 231	2 127	
Europe	1 843	3 434	3 822	2 032	3 105	1 469	1 429	2 142	1 277	2 091	
Others		24	4		115	58	54	5	27	87	
TOTAL	10 378	16 186	17 904	21 152	28 957	37 857	56 678	65 544	59 362	63 998	
Philippines											
Middle East	141 185	132 044	183 582	211 003	323 414	250 210	253 867	236 434	272 038	267 035	241 081
Asia	33 287	17 708	20 322	31 011	40 814	38 817	52 835	72 536	90 434	92 648	86 196
America	11 549	3 534	2 101	3 707	5 646	2 515	3 744	4 035	5 614	7 902	9 962
Europe	7 325	846	1 126	1 465	2 878	3 683	4 067	3 693	5 643	7 614	7 830
Africa	3 427	1 611	2 144	1 098	2 353	1 843	1 977	1 847	1 856	1 958	1 741
Oceania	664	165	223	683	2 072	913	953	1 080	1 271	1 397	1 247
Trust Territory	1 940	1 486	1 438	1 148	3 086	2 397	3 048	3 892	5 373	6 563	7 289
Total (Land based)	199 377	157 394	210 936	250 115	380 263	300 378	320 494	323 517	382 229	385 117	355 346
Seamen	144 411	57 196	55 307	64 169	53 944	50 604	52 290	54 697	67 042	85 913	103 280
TOTAL	343 788	214 590	266 243	314 284	434 207	350 982	372 784	378 214	449 271	471 030	458 626

TABLE 4 (CONTINUED)

Thailand										
Middle East	27 784	20 761	24 638	104 951	64 663	68 229	61 660	74 128	75 113	91 905	87 627
Asia	2 421	723	2 093	3 206	3 814	6 008	7 937	10 621	9 205	21 593	31 536
America							3	562	778	3 240	3 864
Europe	234					448	2	308	205	893	1 056
Others			9	361	35	80	83	43	211	1 326	1 231
TOTAL	30 439	21 484	26 740	108 518	68 512	75 021	69 685	85 662	85 512	118 957	125 314
Bangladesh											
Middle East	68 012	29 815	53 839	62 186	58 229	55 921	76 785	68 004	54 500	67 404	100 432
Asia	133	672	1 083	451	561	801	839	556	296		
Africa	143	2	17	78	42		1		9		
Others	818	84	848	90	384	32	69	98	198	717	1 286
TOTAL	69 106	30 573	55 787	62 805	59 216	56 754	77 694	68 658	55 003	68 121	101 718
India											
Middle East				224 257	217 971	198 520	160 396	109 498	121 812	165 880	120 561
Others				15 288	7 024	7 402	2 639	4 070	3 544	3 964	6 225
TOTAL				239 545	224 995	205 922	163 035	113 568	125 356	169 844	126 786
Pakistan											
Middle East	426 198	115 922	151 522	137 269	119 641	93 434	82 250	57 774	66 076	81 409	
Asia	14	2	2	2		26	10				
Europe	259	6	11	12	9	11	8		31		31
Others	3 456	2 467	1 546	252	381	69	65	228	79		105
TOTAL	429 927	118 397	153 081	137 535	120 031	93 540	82 333	58 002	66 186	81 545	
Sri Lanka											
Middle East	57 300	28 600	57 400	22 450	18 085				15 271	17 793	
Asia									627	989	
Europe									108	164	
Others									121	27	
TOTAL	57 300	28 600	57 400	22 450	18 085	15 753	12 374	15 809	16 127	18 973	11 079

Source: ILO *Statistical Report 1989 International Labour Migration from Asian Labour-Sending Countries*. Bangkok, ILO; C.W. Stahl, "South-North Migration in the Asian-Pacific Region". Paper presented at the Ninth IOM Seminar on Migration, Geneva, 1990. Table 2.
* Figures from 1963-1979.
Reproduced from Lin Lean Lim "The Demographic Situation and Migratory Movements in Asian Countries", a paper presented to the OECD International Conference on Migration, Rome, 1991, Table 6.

TABLE 5

REFUGEE POPULATIONS IN ASIA
1989

Where they are	Nos.	Where they came from	Nos.
Hong Kong	57,000	Viet Nam	57 000
Indonesia	5,100	Viet Nam	5 100
Japan	1,300	Viet Nam	1 300
Malaysia	103,700	Philippines	82 000
		Viet Nam	21 700
Philippines	27,100	Viet Nam	26 100
		Laos	700
		Cambodia	300
Thailand	436,500	Laos	77 700
		Cambodia	320 900
		Burma	21 000
		Viet Nam	16 900
India	294,300	China (Tibet)	100 000
		Sri Lanka	91 500
		Bangladesh	96 000
		Afghanistan	5 200
		Iran	1 400
		Burma	200
Nepal	12,000	China (Tibet)	12 000
Pakistan	3,647,000	Afghanistan	3,622 000
		Iran	25 000

Source: World Refugee Survey, US Committee for Refugees as reported in *The Economist*, 23 December 1989.

TABLE 6

UNITED STATES: IMMIGRANTS ADMITTED BY SELECTED COUNTRY OF BIRTH 1979-89

	1979	1980	1981	1982	1983	1984	1985	1986	1987	1988	1989
Iran	8 476	10 410	11 105	10 314	11 163	13 807	16 071	16 505	14 426	15 246	21 243
Iraq	2 871	2 658	2 535	3 105	2 343	2 930	1 951	1 323	1 072	1 022	1 516
Jordan	3 360	3 322	3 825	2 923	2 718	2 438	2 998	3 081	3 125	3 232	3 921
Kuwait	303	257	317	286	344	437	503	496	507	599	710
Lebanon	4 634	4 136	3 955	3 529	2 941	3 203	3 385	3 994	4 367	4 910	5 716
Syria	1 528	1 658	2 127	2 354	1 683	1 724	1 581	1 604	1 669	2 183	2 675
Yemen	203	160	230	305	268	324	432	420	577	360	831
Egypt	3 241	2 833	3 366	2 800	2 600	2 642	2 802	2 989	3 377	3 016	3 717
Israel	3 093	3 517	3 542	3 356	3 239	3 066	3 113	3 790	3 699	3 640	4 244

Source: United States Department of Commerce, 1989 Statistical Yearbook of the Immigration and Naturalisation Service (United States Dept. of Justice).

TABLE 7

ISRAEL: IMMIGRATION AND COUNTRY OF BIRTH

Region and selected country	15.V.48 to 1951	1952-60	1961-64	1965-71	1972-79	1980-84	1985-89	1990
Asia – of which –	237 704	37 119	19 899	36 309	19 456	7 555	6 878	1 058
Turkey	34 547	6 871	4 793	9 280	3 118	1 604	484	105
Iraq	123 371	2 989	520	1 609	939	81	30	13
Iran	21 910	15 699	8 857	10 645	9 550	3 435	5 052	–
Africa	93 282	143 485	116 671	48 214	19 273	19 356	9 308	4 758
Morocco	28 263	95 945	100 354	30 153	7 780	2 522	1 287	220
Tunisia	13 293	23 569	3 813	7 753	2 148	1 232	710	86
South Africa	666	774	1 003	2 780	5 604	1 362	2 213	174
Ethiopia	10	59	23	75	309	12 575	4 396	4 137
Europe	332 802	106 305	80 788	81 282	183 419	34 604	36 294	189 480
USSR	8 163	13 743	4 646	24 730	137 134	11 549	18 205	184 602
Poland	106 414	39 618	4 731	9 975	6 218	1 884	923	412
Romania	117 950	32 462	63 549	22 635	18 418	7 201	7 406	1 457
America and Oceania	3 822	6 922	10 674	31 726	45 040	21 823	17 546	4 103
USA	1 711	1 553	2 102	16 569	20 963	11 322	7 582	1 248
Argentina	904	2 888	5 537	6 164	13 158	4 815	5 767	2 025
Not Known	20 014	3 307	761	1 504	392	299	170	117
TOTAL	686 739	294 488	228 046	197 821	267 580	83 637	70 196	199 516

Source: Israel Central Bureau of Statistics.

FIGURE 3
PRINCIPAL MIGRATORY MOVEMENTS IN AFRICA

Note: This map shows the general directions of legal and clandestine migration in Africa between 1980 and 1986. The movements indicated by the arrows do not take account of border workers, refugees (see the map in figure 2) or expellees. The thicker arrows indicate particularly large movements, especially in terms of percentage of the population in the country of origin. Three such movements are evident: those from Burkina Faso to Côte d'Ivoire, from Equatorial Guinea to Gabon, and from Ghana to Nigeria. The map highlights several large poles of attraction for migrants: Senegal, Côte d'Ivoire and Nigeria in West Africa; Gabon in Central Africa; Kenya in East Africa; and South Africa in southern Africa. Each of these countries receives immigrants from two or more neighbouring countries. Other countries, such as the Central African Republic, Chad, Guinea, Mali and the United Republic of Tanzania, are a source of migration to more than one neighbouring country.
The boundaries shown on this map have no political significance.

Source: Sergio Ricca, *International Migration in Africa - Legal an Administrative Aspects*, International Labour Office, Geneva, 1989.

3

The Short Road Ahead

The brief overview suggests that widening economic differentials between North and South (and/or limited political freedom and human rights) have not been the main determinants of recent international migration. Economic differentials have almost certainly figured large in the decisions of those who did emigrate, but there is little evidence to suggest that the "mass exodus" scenario, in which millions of poor, deprived people in the South will break through the immigration barriers of the North, is upon us. Indeed, refugee migration, the type closely associated with socio-economic deprivation, limited political freedom and military conflict, has occurred mainly *between* countries of the South. The clearest sign of pressure on the North's immigration barriers has been the increasing number of asylum seekers (who generally enter as visitors and then appeal for status) and illegals (who cross borders often unrestricted and generally work in low-paid jobs).

Most world migration, including a proportion of illegal migration, has been firmly under the control of receiving-governments. Numbers admitted according to type and achievements have been decided by government objectives set for socio-economic growth and these tend to be closely related to a country's stage of modernisation. Of course, governments vary in their application of formal migration regulations, but most have control of their borders, are aware of what is going on, and act swiftly and effectively if it is in their interest to stop or reduce flows or deport illegals.

In attempting to project migration flows for even a short period, one is mindful of the considerable dearth of basic data available and that our knowledge of the causes and consequences of migration is still limited. The modernisation model is still in early stages of development. It seems to apply neatly to the experiences of small countries which have moved rapidly through transition, but a great deal more work is needed to explain the migration/modernisation connection in larger, poorer countries moving slowly through the crucial middle stages of transition. Projection is a hazardous exercise even in the best of circumstances; it is especially hazardous for migration given the diversity of types and differential policies adopted by governments at different stages of development. However, many of the factors that will shape the world economy during the coming decade are already in train or are otherwise sufficiently predetermined to indicate how they will unfold. To the extent that the model is generally robust, then it should point the way to migration flows that will accompany reshaping of the global economy.

One of the main factors already in train is the trend towards greater internationalisation, overlaid on which will be the formation of strengthened *regional* economic blocs. Trade tensions between the major trading nations and more recently the liberation of Eastern Bloc countries, has strengthened the trend towards a new tripolar economic/political grouping - Europe, Asia and the Americas.[1] In 1992, Europe will see many significant changes in standards, interoperability and free movement of goods, capital and labour. Business prospects will improve with the opening up of eastern Europe although the region will almost certainly experience transitional difficulties. In other words, the European economic framework has undergone permanent change; there will/can be no turning back. In the Asian trading block, Japan is the linchpin, although the NICs, initially through foreign investment, have grown very rapidly and there is no reason to suggest that trends will be anything but upward in the short term. It is also highly likely that investors in the region will soon turn their attention to South Asia. In the United States, regional alliances are becoming more important, reflecting perhaps reduced opportunities in Europe post-1992. While the United States is presently dependent on Japan for financing its current account deficit, this could be reduced in the late 1990s as a result of increased savings in the United States flowing from the ageing of its population. The US-Canada Free Trade Agreement, and closer ties with Mexico, Caribbean countries and South America, will be an important feature of that region's future during the next decade.

EUROPE

The migration impacts of these trends will be both important and far reaching for every region of the world. Juhani Lönnroth argues that the challenge of the 1990s for Europe is to recognise the fundamental differences that will occur compared with labour market settings of the past.[2/] Diversification of jobs and markets will be the norm; the era of homogeneous labour markets is over; demand will be for varied skills and qualities, a labour market dominated by service and information technologies. Job-seekers, he predicts, will constantly need to increase their skills. As the IOM South-North seminar in Geneva last year concluded, the question of numbers and skills of immigrants from either eastern Europe or the South is not simply, or even mainly, a supply-side issue; the demand will be for skilled labour with a wide range of specialized knowledge, especially in such fields as machine programming, control and maintenance, and in organisation, co-ordination and managerial functions.[3/] Of major importance for the composition of immigrant labour will be the extent to which ageing receiving-countries initiate approprate programmes of adult education and retraining, and encourage higher workforce-participation rates in an attempt to reduce reliance on immigrant labour. It is a position on which Lönnroth has no doubt: "the core of any labour policy has to be a reliance on domestic labour resources before an import of labour is countenanced". Heinz Werner predicts that even demand for unskilled labour will be met mainly by unemployed EC workers.[4/]

If recognition of new, fundamental differences in the labour market is *the* challenge of the 1990s for Europe, coping with increasing pressures for entry from bordering and nearby countries cannot be far behind. Time and again at recent seminars on international migration we have heard it referred to as "one of the greatest challenges that Europe is going to face" or that the advent of free movement of persons in the European Community post-1992 will "coincide with the greatest increase in immigration pressures that has ever been seen". [5/] While formal labour-market projections suggest that the European Community could, with appropriate policies, remain self-sufficient in terms of filling labour demand, the supply-side issue *vis-à-vis* eastern Europe and the southern Mediterranean (in particular) is unlikely to go away or be resolved by stricter immigration policies.

Some scholars predict that immigration could well be utilised to shore up weaknesses in the education and training systems of countries in the North ; others believe that mounting pressures to emigrate in nearby countries will become an even more important issue. In October 1990, Widgren predicted that if the Soviet Union adopted a "law of free migration", outflows from the East could reach 2.2 million and that further pressure would arise as a result of likely ethnic conflict between Azerbaijan and Armenia.[6/] Flows of this magnitude (which, incidentally, SOPEMI considers unlikely) would certainly verge on "mass exodus". But if receiving-countries admit immigrants in response to a *mix* of labour/demographic requirements, and try to resolve asylum and refugee flows through firmer, more imaginative policies, then the numbers likely to enter western Europe will be fewer and the flows more modulated.

Three scenarios suggested by Jean-Claude Chesnais are worthy of note.[7/] Ethnic migration, which he describes as the regrouping of scattered communities, would certainly impact on sending-countries because many of their potential migrants have well-developed technical skills which, though in demand in the West, would also play a major part in the transition from state-controlled to market economies. He calls the second scenario "political exoduses in the wake of disasters" (persecution of dissidents, ethnic massacres) and identifies Turks in Bulgaria, gypsy populations and minorities in the Soviet Union as being particularly vulnerable. His third scenario is economic migration for survival in which workers in the East, presently earning a fraction of the wages paid for comparable work in the West, will exert strong pressure for migration especially during the period of structural adjustment. The impact of "shock treatment" necessary to change to the market economy could well see 35 to 40 million workers unemployed, but here again, if flows can be firmly regulated by receiving-countries, then those accepted are likely to be highly qualified, young and resourceful persons, especially those with a good knowledge of foreign languages. There is considerable temptation for them to emigrate "in this transitional phase now beginning".

Strong emigration pressures already evident in countries of the southern Mediterranean will, in due course, create what Michele Bruni and Alessandra Venturini have called a "conflictual situation" which could see sending-countries actually encouraging their people to leave.[8/] Demographic projections made by Léon Tabah for nine countries on the southern and eastern Mediterranean indicate that a total population of 69 million in 1950 had reached 189 million in 1990 and was projected to reach 349 million by 2025.[9/] The problem, concluded Tabah, is whether the combination of development and ecological conditions will enable the projected growth to be absorbed into the national economies and how many migrants Europe and other countries will be able to absorb. Whatever happens, there will be increasing pressure to emigrate. Indeed, migrants from this region are already spreading throughout Europe and transforming what were traditional countries of emigration, such as Spain, Italy, Greece and Portugal, into countries of immigration.

Strong though the emigration pressures in eastern Europe and the southern Mediterranean will be during the 1990s, the much larger and generally poorer populations of sub-Saharan Africa and South Asia cannot be ignored by Europe. Already, small communities have been established in parts of western Europe and these can be expected to press strongly for reunification. South Asians in particular are well represented in Europe's known illegal populations.

While emigration from Europe to other regions has declined in recent years, increased world demand for highly qualified and professional workers, especially in the traditional receiving-countries, could see an emigration revival. The globalisation of economic activity in a world described by Allan Findlay as increasingly powered by the activities of transnational corporations,[10/] is likely to result in increased professional transient emigration from Europe, a long-standing major source of such persons.

THE TRADITIONAL RECEIVERS

Because permanent immigration represents such an integral part of the population policies of the United States, Canada and Australia, it is not surprising that each country has already declared its programme for the early 1990s. For 1992 to 1994, the United States will admit, under the 1990 Immigration Act, 714,000 immigrants (excluding refugees) each year and 738,000 each year from 1995 onwards.[11/] This slight increase hides a significant change in composition, namely, an increase in numbers under the "Independent" category from 54,000 a year under current law to 140,000 (including 10,000 Business Migrants yearly) after 1992. A major reason for this change is the expectation of the US Bureau of Labor Statistics that the largest absolute growth in jobs will be in service, professional, administrative and managerial occupations, although Papademetriou rightly warns against making policy decisions on the basis of such projections. A country's long-term competitiveness, he wrote, rests upon its educational and training institutions producing an appropriate workforce, which is the same point made by other scholars concerning western Europe.[12] Yearly entries under the Family Stream will remain at around 480,000 between 1992 and 1994, but are estimated to increase to 543,000 thereafter. Given the large number of former immigrants from developing countries during the last twenty years, it is expected that their relatives will comprise the main share of future immigration under the Family Stream. These will include the relatives of persons who entered the United States illegally but later had their status regularised.

Family members and refugees comprised 70 per cent of *Canada's* immigrants between 1983 and 1985. However, following the findings of a Special Report, Parliament concluded that such a composition was unbalanced relative to the Independent stream which it recommended should be substantially increased. Thus, by 1990 total immigration had increased to 200,000 from 85,000 in 1985 and the share of the Independent stream had increased to 94,000 (i.e., double its share in 1985). The Government's recently adopted five-year Immigration Plan proposes an increase in yearly intake to 250,000 between 1992 and 1995, although numbers entering under the Independent stream will remain at 94,000 a year.[13]

In *Australia*, the influential Fitzgerald Report proposed three immigration scenarios to 2031: annual intakes of 150,000; a gradual increase to 180,000 by 2000 and remaining at that level thereafter; a gradual increase to 220,000 by 2000 also remaining at that level thereafter.[14] Economic recession saw the target for 1991 reduced to 115,000, but intakes are expected to increase to at least the level in the first scenario during the next few years. In addition to retaining the family reunion component at a high level, the Australian Government has indicated its intention of increasing the number of highly-skilled and professional workers under the Independent programme. Given the country's increasing involvement with the Asia-Pacific economic bloc, every effort will be made to attract appropriate immigrants from that region although Europeans, and others with appropriate qualifications, will also be sought.

Each of the traditional receivers will therefore be seeking substantially increased numbers of highly-skilled and professional workers. European countries have also signalled that future demand will be mainly for such persons and that immigration programmes, where these have been articulated, will accord them priority. The trend towards a tripolar economic/political grouping (Europe, Asia and the Pacific and the

Americas), and the fundamental changes in labour-market settings articulated by Lönnroth, will therefore surely combine to create an unusually strong demand for migrants with appropriate skills and experience. Demand is likely to be especially strong during the next few years when education and training institutions adjust their curricula to meet future demand. SOPEMI (1990) has raised important questions concerning the impact of emerging free trade areas in the tripolar regions on migration policies: "Will countries with a shortage of manpower favour a strategy of regional recruitment, or are we about to see, alongside this, fierce competition on a worldwide scale to secure the most highly-skilled workers?".

Short-term immigrant-worker schemes, already well established in the traditional receivers, are unlikely to diminish during the next few years, especially because intakes normally contain executives and professionals who spend short periods of employment in one of their company's, or a joint-venture's, regional office. Family reunion components of permanent immigration will clearly favour persons from countries which have recently provided first or early 'links' in migration chains. The United States can therefore expect to see little change in the dominance of Central and South America and Asia in its family stream, and Australia little change in the increasing importance of Asia.

There is little doubt that each of the traditional receivers, such as western Europe, will face increased numbers of asylum seekers and illegal migrants. Widgren has warned that they are "quickly heading for a serious crisis" and that a clear tendency is emerging towards the collapse of asylum systems.[15/] Proposals for change range from the Swedish proposal for better coordination of foreign policy to include development cooperation, refugee and immigration policies, to those which seek firmer application of existing regulations. David North has argued that democracies such as the United States do not control migration well because they are reluctant to devote the needed financial, diplomatic, intellectual and, above all, the emotional resources to the issue.[16/] And the Australian Government's paper tabled at the IOM South-North Seminar in December 1990 contained a strong recommendation that appropriate *international* machinery be established to assist in the resolution of many contemporary problems concerning asylum seekers and illegal migrants.

CENTRAL AND SOUTH AMERICA

Given this region's poor economic growth performance in recent years, significant changes are unlikely to occur during the early 1990s. Intra-continental flows which bring large numbers of poor people from rural areas and across borders to nearby urban areas will continue until the economic/ demographic conditions which cause such flows are resolved. Migration to the United States, if only through family reunification, will continue for some time and new US policy concerning Independent migration will exacerbate the well-established braindrain. Rodrigo Escobar-Navia holds the view that even if US initiatives to make the continent a free-trade community or zone succeed, traditional South-North migration will continue, a view supported by the Lattes primarily on the grounds of present economic conditions. Nor is the interest being shown by young Latin Americans to use their ethnic backgrounds as a medium for entering Europe likely to subside. John Salt argues that the potential for such emigration is considerable in view of the large stock of persons of Spanish and Portuguese origin in Latin America.

ASIA

Rapid rates of economic growth in Japan and the "four dragons" have already had significant employment and investment multiplier effects on other countries in east and southeast Asia, especially high labour demand which cannot be met from local supplies. Lin Lean Lim considers that the economic integration of Asia and Pacific rim countries is perhaps the most significant development that will affect future migration flows. There has already been progressive relocation of labour-intensive production away from the more technically-advanced Asian countries to others with cheap and expanding labour supplies. Hong Kong and Singapore have been encouraging their nationals to exploit such opportunities as one way of dealing with labour shortages. Countries which have already gone through transition, and those rapidly doing so, will increasingly opt for the "relocation" option, and those at early stages of transition will continue to provide the labour for service-type jobs that cannot be exported. Growing inter-country inequalities within the region, in combination with increasing economic integration, will ensure that both capital-assisted and non-capital assisted migration will increase over time. The question is no longer whether the rapidly developing countries of the region should admit foreign manpower but, writes Stahl, on what terms they are admitted, what rights they have and the welfare measures to which they are entitled.[17]

Thus, while Asia as a whole is joining the Middle East as a major destination of Asian migrant workers, probably over half the estimated one million foreign workers in the four main labour-importing countries are illegal.[18] Primarily because of its sustained high economic growth rates and sub-replacement fertility, Japan is expected to become a prime target for such workers during the 1990s. Once decisions have been made concerning capital-intensive production, local workforce participation rates and degree of job export, we will have a better idea of the numbers of foreign workers likely to be needed but, according to Philip Martin, Japan seems less confident than Singapore that it can rotate migrants and therefore prevent settlement. Steps have already been taken to impose heavy penalties on the employers of illegals, and a high-level study group has been established to look at, among other things, ways of attaining macro supply-demand balance without relying on foreign workers.[19]

Similar questions face other governments in the region. Taiwan represents a "vast potential for employment" in the construction, textile, transport and hotel industries, and Thailand, Indonesia, Malaysia and South Korea, are showing demand for more workers in particular sectors.[20] As with Europe, the supply-side poses no constraint. The Philippines and Indonesia will remain important suppliers of labour to both nearby and Middle East markets in the short term, and South Asia is also an enormous reservoir. The toe-holds already established by migrant workers from Bangladesh and Pakistan will almost certainly be strengthened by the arrival of others. And, as has often been noted, if the People's Republic of China lifted restrictions on emigration, it could provide all and more of the workers required even if all countries opted for foreign labour as the main solution for their labour shortages.

MIDDLE EAST AND SOUTH ASIA

Although Middle East oil-producers will remain major receivers of foreign labour in the forseeable future, further changes in composition will almost certainly occur. A shift in demand away from construction to more highly-skilled and service workers has already occurred. The uncertainty introduced into the region's labour market by the Gulf crisis has undermined confidence in the market's stability. Suggestions that Egypt may become the main future source of both skilled and semi-skilled labour for Kuwait have been received with alarm in Asian supply countries, though presumedly not in Egypt. The Middle East has been, and will continue to be, a major source of remittance-income for countries of supply. Sending-governments have understandably built into their forward estimates of export earnings remittance payments similar to those received in the recent past. A major shortfall in budgeted income would undermine development strategies that rely upon hard-currency earnings.

Table 4 indicates that contract labour from South Asia was sustained at high levels throughout the 1980s. While changing composition of demand will be met more easily by countries with appropriate industrial sectors and therefore skill compositions, the region's generally low per capita income, and high rates of population growth pose economic problems that labour exports alone cannot resolve.

SUB-SAHARAN AFRICA

Together with South Asia, sub-Saharan Africa provides the main challenge for economic development. With a network of countries mostly at early stages of demographic transition, and with no established outlets for either migrant workers in labour-scarce regions or for refugees, migration has been dominated by intra-regional flows between countries at medium to low stages of development. Nor can one expect greatly-improved rates of economic growth during the 1990s. Neither unemployment/ underemployment nor inequality and poverty have been reduced over the past decade, a prospect that Adepoju sees as a "major bottleneck to the attainment of egalitarian societies".[21/] The prospects for economic recovery in Africa in the next decade are bleak. There are pointers that even the traditional labour-importing, relatively rich countries (Gabon and Côte d'Ivoire), and recent attractive destinations for migrants such as Zimbabwe and Nigeria, are at different stages of economic crisis that not only render them incapable of attracting migrants, but might even spur out-migration of their own nationals.

Adepoju is not alone in his view that bleak economic prospects will trigger migration within countries in sub-Saharan Africa and to other regions. The Swedish Study

Group predicts a rising disposition to migrate and cites Nigeria as a country facing serious economic/demographic pressures as its population increases from 100 million to 150 million in only 10 years. And Widgren believes that the small but growing sub-Sahara communities in Europe will act as important bridgeheads for further immigration. Russell, *et al.*, while acknowledging the existence and potential importance of policy measures governing international migration , caution against concluding from such evidence that the volume and importance of migration will necessarily decline. Indeed, their overall review of evidence that they so meticulously assembled and assessed was that the volume of international migration will not be substantially reduced in the near future.

NOTES

1.
Henry Ergas and Paul Paterson, "The World Economy to the Year 2020", a chapter in R. T. Appleyard (Ed.), ***Western Australia into the Twenty-First Century: Economic Perspectives,*** Perth, West Australia, 1991, pp. 21-38.
2.
J. Lönnroth, op. cit., pp. 7-9.
3.
R. T. Appleyard, "Summary Report of the Rapporteur", *International Migration*, Vol. XXIX, No. 2, June 1991, p. 336.
4.
Heinz Werner, op. cit., p. 9.
5.
A. Kuijsten, op. cit., p. 22; D. Coleman, op. cit., p. 2.
6.
Jonas Widgren , *International Affairs* article, 1990, p. 757.
7.
Jean-Claude Chesnais, "Migration from Eastern to Western Europe, past (1946-1989) and future (1990-2000)", Council of Europe, Conference of Ministers on the Movement of persons coming from Central and Eastern European countries (Vienna, 24-25 January 1991), Strasbourg 1991, pp. 20-5.
8.
N. Bruni and A. Venturini, op. cit., pp. 9-10.
9.
Léon Tabah, "Demographic Imbalances between the Countries of the Mediterranean Basin", a Report to the Council of Europe, Committee on Migration, Refugees and Demography, Strasbourg, April 1991.
10.
Allan M. Findlay, "New Technology, High Level Manpower Movements and the Concept of the Brain Drain", a paper presented at the OECD International Conference on Migration, Rome, March 1991, p. 4.
11.
Demetrios Papademetriou, Geneva paper, Table 1, p. 10B.
12.
Demetrios Papademetriou, *International Migration*, Vol. XXIX, No. 2, June 1991, pp. 299-300.
13.
Mildred J. Morton, op. cit.

14.
Australia, Immigration. *A Committment to Australia,* The Report of the Committee to Advise on Australia's Immigration policies, AGPS, Canberra, 1988.
15.
Jonas Widgren, OECD paper, 1991, p. 9.
16.
David North, "Why Democratic Governments cannot cope with Illegal Immigration", a paper presented at the OECD International Conference on Migration, Rome, March 1991, p. 4.
17.
C. W. Stahl, op. cit., p. 16.
18.
Martin, op. cit., p. 190.
19.
Lin Lean Lim, Geneva paper, pp. 46-7.
20.
J.N. Sarmiento, op. cit., p. 200.
21.
A. Adepoju, op. cit., p. 216.

4

The Long View

Although the Swedish Study Group has provided a timely warning for anyone planning to predict migration flows for more than a few years ahead ("It is impossible to arrive at scientifically tenable forecasts of future migrant and refugee flows"), they did concede that it was possible to "identify tendencies". Yet even tendencies can be quickly redirected by major, unexpected political events such as the recent break-up of the Soviet Union.

As already noted, the main parameters for international migration into the 21st century have already been set by the trend towards greater internationalism overlaid on which will be the formation of strengthened regional economic blocs, and the recent liberation of Eastern Bloc countries has only strengthened the trend towards a new tripolar economic/political grouping. The countervailing factor in this scenario is, of course, the Third World and how countries and regions presently, but not necessarily permanently, outside the tripolar grouping will be affected by their activities, especially the extent to which, and under what terms, their human and physical resources will be utilised by the tripolars.

While migration tendencies will therefore be shaped mainly by this "dualistic" global setting, it would be foolish to suggest that the composition of each bloc, and even the composition of the respective tripolars, will not change. A brief reflection on global economic and political trends during the last forty years should be sufficient to deter anyone from holding that view. Should the Soviet Union's substantial natural resources be exploited partly, or even mainly, by capital from the west, there could be considerable capital-assisted migration, mainly professional transients moving between the Soviet Union and countries of the North. And if the People's Republic of China eased restrictions on family size and emigration, the impact on global population growth and migration flows would be considerable.

The widening gap in socio-economic differentials between North and South, and the almost certain prospect that global population will increase to over 11 billion during the 21st century, is set to exacerbate disagreement and conflict. Over 90 per cent of the projected population will be living outside the tripolar groupings, mainly in countries presently experiencing low and declining standards of living. Many of the migration options noted in Chapter 3 took no account of long-term scenarios; instead they were directed towards how migration would facilitate the economic growth of both sending- and receiving-countries in the short term, and the conditions under which asylum seeker and illegal migration could be controlled. However, as Elmar Hönnekop has warned, countries of the North will not be able to shut themselves completely from the demographic differentials between the North and the South and will have to work out "important complementary strategies in the field of economic co-operation". [1] Such strategies will need to extend beyond utilising the South's physical and human resources for the North's economic benefit.

There is now general consensus that the South-North predicament cannot, nor ever could, be solved through emigration *per se*. The orders of magnitude, as A. Golini's research has shown, are too large; nor would countries of the North open their gates to all-comers. Five North African countries alone will increase their populations threefold by 2025 and, as G. Tapinos has rightly concluded, it would require a "veritable economic revolution for the national (European) labour markets to be able to absorb such an increase in numbers".[2] Even if some western countries decided to increase substantially immigration as one means of arresting demographic decline (and the OECD has warned that this is not so easy a "solution" as sometimes thought),[3] intakes would almost certainly be selective (young, skilled workers and their families), and numbers suggested would have no noticeable effect on North-South demographic differentials.* Demographic transition implies that, by the late 21st

---

* H. Zlotnik has shown that in order to prevent population decline in the European Community during the first half of the 21st century, an estimated one million immigrants a year would be required.[4]

century, fertility levels in developing countries will have declined substantially. However, the predicament for the next fifty years, while so many demographic heavyweights move through the second and third stages of transition, is that little if anything can happen to prevent the global population from reaching the projected ten billion or more.

In the absence of appropriate global economic policies which address the enormous income gap between North and South, problems that are symptomatic of the dilemma are unlikely to be resolved. The number of asylum seekers and illegal migrants will therefore almost certainly increase. The propensity for receiving-governments to look for solutions through tighter border controls or through deportation if applications have been rejected, is understandable. But the asylum-seeker/illegal issue will only be resolved by tackling the situations that largely caused it to occur. Widgren has called for new policies to address the current influx of asylum seekers in OECD European countries and has warned that, in their absence, the numbers could well exceed the number of regular migrants within a few years.[5] Time is running out, he wrote, and solutions are urgently needed to avoid breakdown of the whole institution of asylum. Tighter border controls or annual quotas are directed towards stabilising and controlling the recent rapid increase in numbers; they are not directed towards long-term solutions. Asylum seekers have exploited loopholes in the formal immigration regulations because those regulations prevented their entry.

The Swedish Study Group is one of the few to have carefully studied and then proposed viable long-term solutions to the asylum seeker/illegal and refugee problems. Calling for a holistic approach to the North-South dilemma, the Group proposed that government foreign policy should be *co-ordinated* to encompass development co-operation, refugee and immigration policies. New mechanisms and new solutions to migratory pressures from the Third World countries should be directed towards facilitating the economic and social development of those countries. Indeed, migratory movements could well be stimulated by development programmes without forcing migrants into the "asylum fold".

Just as there is general consensus that resolution of the North-South dilemma is not mass migration, so there is growing consensus that the Swedish approach (facilitating economic and social development) is a durable solution. There is no reason for believing, argue the Swedes, that migratory pressure on Europe and other OECD countries will diminish until the "gap" between North and South is substantially reduced. This can only be achieved, in their view, by "measures that support sustainable development", although they rightly warn that rapid economic development also causes greater mobility and an acceleration of the urbanisation process which, in turn, augments migration potential. SOPEMI (1990) has also concluded, bluntly, that "the real issue is underdevelopment", not emigration, and called for a new form of co-operation between North and South directed to reducing *incentives* to emigrate from South countries. And the *Human Development Report for 1991* firmly concluded that the best way to promote human development is through more equitable growth and participatory government, a view echoed by the Brundtland Report of 1987.

In citing Africa as a major problem area, Papademetriou argued that it will be only in policies that address the less-developed societies populations' need for survival, as well as aspirations for economic mobility, that progress towards the long-term control of unauthorised migration can be made.[6/] And Tapinos put the issue well when he observed that the impact of international co-operation as an alternative to emigration, at least has the merit of highlighting the fact that the problem of migration is *secondary* to that of development. Development, he claimed, is the only path possible in the longer term.[7/]

Development strategies that effectively address North-South differentials at a time when tripolar economic/political groupings are being formed and strengthened, will not be easily or readily devised. The South encompasses a myriad of economic/political situations and appropriate strategies for each country would vary enormously. Initiatives from the North would therefore need to be directed towards creating a global economic environment favourable to countries at all stages of modernisation or demographic transition.

The four aspects of a development package necessary to create such an environment are trade, debt relief, investment and co-operative aid. In identifying international trade as the single most effective means of securing responsiveness to changing opportunities, Soltwedel argued that action designed to strengthen and extend the open multilateral trading system - both by OECD and developing countries - is the key to improving living standards.[8/] The World Bank has also declared that the outcome of the Uruguay Round of trade talks is critical to the future of the multilateral trading system and the welfare of the whole world community. The emergence of regional trading arrangements (tripolar economic/political groupings) could pose dangers to multilateral trade liberalisation, although this need not be the case. If it does, the Bank foresees diminishing long-term global prospects with developing countries outside the blocs likely to be "hurt severely".[9] Similar concerns about the failure of the Uruguay Round and the movement towards economic blocs were expressed by the *Human Development Report for 1991*. Present barriers to trade, unless reduced, were seen as one of the main issues likely to lead to an increase in South-North migration.

Improved access to markets of developed countries is regarded as a crucial aspect of the economic development of countries in the South. This was certainly the conclusion reached by the US Commission for the Study of International Migration and Economic Development concerning the future of Central America. It urged the US Government to expedite the development of a US-Mexico free-trade area and "encourage its incorporation with Canada into a North American free-trade area".[10] While this would be an ideal solution for Mexico and other countries incorporated into the area, it would not effectively address the broader tripolar *versus* others (developing countries) issue which is the purpose of the Uruguay Round. But if, as Soltwedel proposes, regional integration is in line with objectives for maintaining and strengthening the open multilateral trading system, and in conformity with international obligations, then it could be an effective medium for achieving the broader objectives. It should, however, be emphasised that the abandonment of long-standing restrictive trade and investment policies in both developed and developing countries will not be easily achieved unless both groups are assured that the new arrangements will enhance- their situations. The long and tortuous discussions so far, and the seemingly-entrenched positions taken by several groups, cannot encourage the governments of the South. Yet El Mouhoub Mouhoud is optimistic: a "true policy of co-operation" at the level of international agreements through the General Ageement on Tariffs and Trade, and preferential agreements between certain industrialised and developing countries has, he suggests, the potential for improving the competetiveness of firms in industrialised countries and enhancing the chances of development for Third World countries.[11]

The magnitude of accumulated external debt in developing countries is enormous. Burden of debt together with the reversal of net resource transfers, constitute fundamental obstacles for human development. By the end of 1990, Latin American countries alone had accumulated $ 423 billion in long-term loans outstanding and were paying out 24 per cent of their export earnings to service the debt. This had greatly reduced hard-currency earnings necessary to acquire capital equipment to improve productivity in the domestic sector. Although total debt in African countries is much less than in Latin America, the relative burden is more severe. In low-income countries on that continent, debt is typically five times annual export income, and, for ten countries, debt servicing averages 80 per cent of export income. Most of the debt has been accumulated by governments and in recent years focus has shifted from rescheduling to service reduction, including schemes for debt conversion, debt buy-backs and special bonds. Even so, debt remains one of the prime obstacles to economic and social growth in developing countries. Its relief is deemed by many economists as essential to restoring conditions for economic growth.

Debt problems have also seriously affected foreign direct investment in countries of the South during the last decade.[12/] They have recently been receiving a falling share of total inward investment, in sharp contrast with the second half of the 1970s, and there is now much greater reliance placed upon direct investment "packages". According to SOPEMI (1990), the downturn in direct investment and in volume of trade with the South is primarily the result of the growing indebtedness of the majority of developing countries and of the poor prospects that some of these countries offer in terms of return on investment. With the advent of the debt crisis, international lending fell and the international market for securities began to "grow vigorously".[13/] Most developing countries are no longer able to borrow from external commercial sources and so most of the one trillion dollars gross capital flows in 1987 were *between* industrial countries. Net transfers to developing countries declined from $ 37 billion in 1980 to a negative $ one billion in 1989, and access to the international securities market for many developing countries became limited.

While it is widely acknowledged that the North should open up their markets and provide international investment consistent with development assistance in order to prevent low-income countries from "further drifting away from the mainstream of the world economy", [14/] it is also generally agreed that the receiving countries have a responsibility for creating the "right environment". A stable macro environment is a *necessary* condition for growth to occur. Co-operative aid and development assistance loom large in most proposals for the early stages of economic reconstruction and reform. Marshall Plan-type aid has occasionally been suggested as an appropriate approach in view of the magnitude of the North-South economic divide. The US Commission certainly saw aid and development assistance, together with relaxation of trade barriers, as key aspects of any development strategy especially if (as Tapinos shrewdly observed) it appeared to be in the interests of industrialised countries. An increase in aid by EC countries to 1 per cent of GNP would yield an estimated $ 62 billion per year between 1993 and 2000.[15/] If only half of this was directed to the South and effectively was then utilised to facilitate an overall development package, the impact on the South-North divide, and in due course on emigration pressure, would be considerable.

To what extent, and in what ways, could international migration be factored into development packages that addressed trade, debt, investment and co-operative aid? So much attention seems to have been devoted to ruminating over the mass exodus scenario (which, it is generally agreed, cannot be the answer to the "demographic challenge of the South"),[16/] that little attention has been given to the positive role that international migration could play in an overall development strategy. Obviously, its role in specific countries would vary according to their stages of modernisation. Factoring migration into development strategies that are appropriate for many countries in sub-Saharan Africa and South Asia would clearly be a more challenging and demanding exercise than factoring it into the development policies of Asian NICs. Capital-assisted migration, involving many professional transients, would play a key role in countries at early stages of renewed economic growth, but investors would need to be assured that the economic and political climate in the receiving- countries was favourable for such transfers.

With improved economic growth, "exchange" of migrants would, as the transition model shows, reflect each country's stage and rate of economic growth. In addition to professional transients moving to countries of the South, there would also be a flow of selected workers moving from receiving-countries to institutions or factories in developed countries for appropriate training. Flows of this kind have been common, especially from countries moving rapidly through transition and unable to provide numbers of needed skilled/professional workers from indigenous institutions not organised for such output. The new era would see a significant increase in such flows and possibly a lower incidence of wastage as trainees had more incentive to return home where job opportunities had been created by the successful development package. Böhning refers to this as "migration for training" not for the purpose of employment in the countries of the North but with a view to picking up skills for employment in their home countries to which they would return and become economically active.[17/]

If the transition model is reasonably robust, then migration would increase markedly between countries at different stages of economic evolution. The emergence of tripolars is a new development and account would need to be taken of their possible dominance over economic development and restructuring. Note should also be taken of the US Commission's timely warning not only that there is no simple relationship between migration and development, but also that in the short-term (30 to 40 years), rapid and successful economic development has a profoundly destabilising effect on developing countries. It tends to *increase* migration rather than moderate it even though in the long run it reduces emigration pressures which nowadays is a topic of such concern in many developed countries.

Given economic and political conditions in many parts of the South, refugee migration as a result of processes described by Zolberg, *et al.*, could not be avoided even during early stages of the new development strategy. The conditions for their manifestation have already been created in many places, and spin-off from the development strategy would be too late to prevent the worsening of some refugee situations and the creation of others. Yet there is little doubt that in the long run the development approach offers real promise for restraining refugee flows and reducing broader emigration pressures.

One must, however, be realistic concerning the chances of an appropriate global development strategy being adopted. Development as a medium for reducing economic differentials, and therefore emigration pressure, is not a new proposal, although progressive deterioration of economic conditions in many parts of the South has given the situation a new and increasing sense of urgency. Meantime, international migration will continue to facilitate both economic development and, in its several clandestine/illegal forms, remain a difficult and polemical issue in the North. Thus Lönnroth's plea for a labour-market strategy for international migration to include co-ordination with strategies to develop economic and human potential in sending countries need not await the adoption of a new global development strategy. Likewise, relocating production, creating joint ventures and investing in labour-surplus countries are options that have been, and will continue to be, mutually beneficial to investor and receiver.

While development would, in many respects, be a self-serving option for the North, it is the only viable approach to resolving the North-South dilemma, including those inequalities that are legacies of past policies. Raising immigration barriers alone is no durable solution for, in the absence of a development strategy, income differentials would continue to widen and emigration pressures increase. Without carefully-planned development, there will almost certainly be a deterioration in the physical environments of many developing countries. The human environment in many countries of the South is already unsustainable. Rural poverty in Africa and Asia has doubled since 1950. Together with population pressures, it often forces people to cultivate even more marginal lands which further erodes the thin soil and depletes shallow water resources. Nearly one billion people already live on drylands being affected by increasing desertification. Lack of water has forced people to move; according to Sadik an estimated 1.7 billion people, spread among 80 countries, are already suffering water shortages.[18] Contrariwise, over-abundance of water, often caused by deforestation of upland watersheds, can and has caused severe floods in lowland regions/countries such as Bangladesh.

The case for much more reflection, dialogue and action on the global alternatives to mass migration is strong and proven. There is, as Widgren claims, no serious, systematic thinking taking place at the international level on the linkage between large-scale internal and international migration, population increase, regional inequality and global security. Of equal concern is dearth of information and analysis on both the magnitude and causes of international migration and how these interact with other global problems and may interact in the future. We are, wrote Papademetriou, still quite inept in understanding the linkages between development of the countries of worker-origin and the various internal and external policies that can have a significant impact on it.[19] Maintaining the *status quo* is the best way to invite the next wave of international migration into the OECD countries which, in turn, would further stimulate extreme political reactions.[20] What is needed is an *active* policy with respect to international migration and not just a passive *ad hoc* reaction to events as they materialise. A comprehensive development strategy in which international migration is assigned a specific role, represents the most promising direction.

NOTES

1.
Elmar Hönekopp, "East-West Migration: Recent Developments," a paper presented at the OECD International Conference on Migration, Rome, March 1991, p. 16.

2.
G. Tapinos, op. cit., p. 7.

3.
OECD, *Migration. The Demographic Aspects*, Paris, 1991.

4.
H. Zlotnik, Rome OECD paper, p. 10.

5.
J. Widgren, *International Affairs* article, p. 763.

6.
D. Papademetriou, Rome OECD paper, p. 6.

7.
G. Tapinos, op. cit., p. 12.

8.
R. Soltwedel, op. cit., p. 9.

9.
World Bank, *Global Economic Prospects and the Developing Countries,* Washington, D. C., May 1991, p. 2.

10.
US Commission for the Study of International Migration and Co-operative Economic Development, *Unauthorised Migration: Addressing the Root Causes,* 3 volumes, 1990, p. XVIII.

11.
El M. Mouhoud, op. cit., pp. 16-17.

12.
Jean-Luc Le Bideau, "The Economic Climate for Foreign Direct Investment", a paper presented at the OECD International Conference on Migration, Rome, March 1991, p. 8.

13.
World Bank, op. cit., p. 12.

14.
L. Emmerij, op. cit., p. 12.

15.
Ibid., p. 12.

16.
D. Papademetriou, *International Migration* article, p. 241.

17.
W. R. Böhning, "International Migration to Western Europe: What to do?", a paper presented to the Seminar on International Security, The Graduate Institute of International Studies, Geneva, 15-20 July 1991, p. 13.

18.
N. Sadik, The State of World Population, p. 11.

19.
D. Papademetriou, Rome OECD paper, p. 30.

20.
L. Emmerij, op. cit., p. 14.

Printed in Switzerland by Imprimerie Genevoise SA, Geneva
November 1991

ISBN: 92-9068-036-9